Strike Force

Strike Force

THE USAF IN BRITAIN SINCE 1948

ROBERT JACKSON

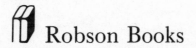 Robson Books

First published in Great Britain in 1986 by Robson Books Ltd.,
Bolsover House, 5–6 Clipstone Street, London W1P 7EB.

British Library Cataloguing in Publication Data

Jackson, Robert
  Strike Force.
  1. United States, *Air Force* — History
  2. United States — Armed Forces
  Great Britain — History
  I. Title
  358.4'00973   UG633

  ISBN 0-86051-303-3

Printed in the United Kingdom by St Edmondsbury Press,
Bury St Edmonds, Suffolk

Contents

Acknowledgments

I should like to thank the USAF Information Services at Mildenhall, Lakenheath, Upper Heyford and Alconbury for providing material that greatly assisted in the preparation of this book. My thanks also go to Bill Gunston for supplying material on the F-111, and I have referred to his own book on that aircraft (*General Dynamics F-111*, Ian Allan Ltd, 1978); to Alan Todd and Colin Lambert, who supplied photographs; and to Angela Tunstall, who painstakingly compiled the detailed list of USAF bases contained in the Appendix. To anyone wishing to have a wider view of USAF operations worldwide I recommend *The History of the US Air Force* by Bill Yenne (Hamlyn, 1984), an admirably illustrated and detailed work of reference.

Introduction

On 17 August, 1942, American heavy bombers took off from British airfields to attack targets in Occupied Europe for the first time. Just a few months later, the USAAF's bomber force in Britain had been transformed into one of the mightiest war machines the world had ever seen, and one which greatly contributed to the ultimate Allied victory.

In the months after the Second World War that great machine was dismantled just as quickly as it had been created, and by the end of 1945 the airfields that had sprung up all over East Anglia and the Midlands lay deserted. Yet within three years the Americans were back, this time to face a different threat, and they have been here ever since.

The aim of this book is to examine the activities of the United States Air Force in Britain over the past four decades, in the wider context of European and world strategy. It seeks to show how operational concepts have changed, and are continuing to change in the light of new military technology on both sides of the Iron Curtain. It is not, nor is it intended to be, a political essay; where political comment exists, it does so to explain and expand on operational aspects.

There is, however, one underlying theme that will be plain from the outset. It is that Western Europe, or at any rate a large slice of it, would probably not have survived in freedom if the Americans had not returned in those critical post-war years. The message should be plain, too: that when the nations of Western Europe are strong enough, and wise enough, to stand solidly together, then will be the time for the Americans to withdraw. But not until then.

R.J., 1986

UNITED STATES AIR FORCE BASES IN BRITAIN
1945-85

KIRKNEWTON

PRESTWICK

AYR

FULL SUTTON

ELVINGTON

BURTONWOOD

LINDHOLME

SCAMPTON

SEALAND

EAST KIRBY

SCULTHORPE

FOULSHAM

BRUNTINGTHORPE   ALCONBURY   MARHAM

MOLESWORTH   LAKENHEATH

CHELVESTON   MILDENHALL

WITCHFORD

BASSINGBOURN   BENTWATERS

UPPER HEYFORD   WOODBRIDGE

BRIZE NORTON   CHICKSANDS   WETHERSFIELD

STANSTED

FAIRFORD   BOVINGDON   MANSTON

WELFORD

GREENHAM COMMON

1

A Question of Strategy, 1945–47

ONE DAY IN the spring of 1946 the inhabitants of Downham Market and its surrounding villages in the flat fenlands of Norfolk looked up as the roar of aero-engines split the sky. It was not the sound made by the Rolls-Royce Merlins of the Avro Lincolns used by the RAF's Central Bomber Establishment at nearby Marham aerodrome, and no wonder; the three great silver aircraft that slid one by one down the approach to Marham's runway were Boeing B-29 Superfortresses, the most advanced strategic bombers in service anywhere in the world. Aircraft such as these had carried atomic bombs to Hiroshima and Nagasaki.

The United States Army Air Force squadrons that had filled the skies of East Anglia with the thunder of their engines were gone now; the airfields occupied for three years by the Fortresses and Liberators, Marauders and Mitchells, Mustangs, Thunderbolts and Lightnings that had trailed their chalkmarks over the Third Reich either lay derelict or had been handed over to the Royal Air Force. Honington, in Suffolk, had been the last to be relinquished; the 364th Fighter Group had flown its P-51D Mustangs back to the USA in November 1945, and three months later the base had been returned to the RAF for use by Transport Command.

The arrival of the B-29s at Marham — along with seven B-17 Flying Fortresses, with whose outlines the people of East Anglia had grown so familiar in the war years — caused considerable excitement and gave rise to speculation that the Americans might have come back to stay. However, they were there for only a short time, having flown to England to take part in Operation Ruby — a programme of weapons trials with deep-penetration bombs against former enemy U-Boat pens and other targets, carried out in conjunction with the RAF's Central Bomber Establishment. While the latter's Lincolns and Lancasters carpeted Heligoland with 12,000-pound Tallboy and 22,000-pound Grand Slam bombs, the B-29s and B-17s used guided bombs in the VB (Vertical Bomb) series against the U-Boat pens at Farge. (The trials contributed to the development of the 2,000-pound VB-4 Razon and 12,000-pound VB-13 Tarzon bombs, which were used successfully against difficult targets such as reservoirs and bridges in the Korean War.)

RAF Marham was to see more B-29s in 1947, when Superfortresses of the 97th Bomb Group paid a courtesy visit, but it was a rare occurrence; the great strategic bombing machine that had helped bring Germany and Japan to their knees was in the process of being dismantled. The combination of B-29 and atomic bomb had turned the USAAF into America's first line of defence — a position traditionally held by the US Navy — almost overnight, and there had been talk since April 1945 of establishing a new-look Air Force on a co-equal basis with the Army and Navy under a single Department of National Defense.

The precedent had been set in 1944, when the US Joint Chiefs of Staff had created an autonomous air force, the Twentieth, to undertake the strategic air offensive against Japan. Operating first from bases in southern China, and later from the Marianas, the Twentieth AF's B-29s had set about the systematic destruction of Japan's industrial cities, culminating in the dropping of the two atomic bombs.

The architect of the independent United States Air Force was General H.H. 'Hap' Arnold, who had been working steadily towards that goal since he became head of the US Army Air Corps in 1938 and in 1941 had presided over the creation of the United States Army Air Force. By the end of 1945, however, with his goal almost in sight, Arnold's health was failing — the stress of his wartime duty had brought on a series of heart attacks — and on 28 February 1946 he retired, handing over command of the USAAF to General Carl Spaatz. During the war, as Arnold's subordinate, Spaatz had commanded the US Strategic Air Forces in the European Theatre and had worked closely with Air Chief Marshal Sir Arthur Harris, C-in-C RAF Bomber Command, in prosecuting the bombing offensive against Germany by day and night.

Spaatz had the basic structure with which to mould the USAAF into a separate entity, but he was sadly lacking in the necessary equipment. At the end of the war with Germany the force had reached a peak strength of 2,282,259 personnel, but rapid demobilisation had reduced the number to 890,000 by the end of 1945 and by February 1946 the total had almost halved again to 450,000. The aircraft that had carried the war to the enemy were being scrapped or sold off in their thousands; only the B-29 force remained relatively intact, because the B-29 was the only American aircraft capable of carrying the atomic bomb.

The first step towards the establishment of a separate air force was taken on 21 March 1946, when three new USAAF Commands — Strategic, Tactical and Air Defense — were formed in the United States. The Strategic Air Command, with its nuclear-armed B-29s, was the 'teeth'; its nucleus was the Second Air Force, soon joined by the Eighth and Fifteenth Air Forces on their return from Europe. The Ninth Air Force, also returning from Europe, was assigned to the Tactical Air Command.

The United States Air Force officially came into being on 26 July 1947, and on 26 September General Spaatz was sworn in as its first Chief of Staff, with General Hoyt Vandenberg as his deputy. On 1 October the Eleventh Air Force became the Alaskan Air Command, guarding the area from which any future threat to the United States was likely to come, and a little later the air units assigned to the occupation forces in Europe became the United States Air Forces Europe (USAFE), the organisation that is central to the theme of this book.

Meanwhile, cuts in personnel and aircraft strengths had continued to take their toll. At the end of 1947 the Strategic Air Command, the strongest of any, had only 319 B-29s and 350 fighters, about half of the latter being Lockheed P-80 Shooting Star jets; most fighter squadrons were still equipped with the

P-51 Mustang. By this time personnel strength had fallen to just under 306,000, less than that of the USAAF at the time of the Japanese attack on Pearl Harbor in December 1941. On the other side of the Atlantic RAF Bomber Command, DSC's equivalent, was in even worse shape; the majority of the squadrons that had hammered Germany night after night had been disbanded, and of those that remained in September 1947 six were still equipped with Avro Lancasters while the other fourteen had Lincolns — a total of about 230 aircraft.

It is interesting at this point to compare the relative capabilities of the principal bombers of the USAF and RAF, because this was a factor that was to have no small bearing on future USAF involvement in Britain. At the beginning of 1947 the British Government under Prime Minister Clement Attlee had decided that Britain was to manufacture her own nuclear weapons; the Air Staff, under the chairmanship of Lord Tedder, had drafted a specification for such a weapon and the aircraft to carry it. The aircraft would eventually emerge as the RAF's trio of V-Bombers — Valiant, Vulcan and Victor — and the bomb would reach operational form as the 24-foot, 10,000-pound Blue Danube, but not until the mid-1950s; in the meantime Bomber Command was left seriously lacking in striking power.

The principal RAF heavy bomber of the late 1940s, the Avro Lincoln, had first flown in 1944 and was a product of the British policy of developing existing designs to the limit, rather than seeking new and revolutionary breakthroughs. So the Lincoln was a straightforward development of its illustrious predecessor, the Avro Lancaster, and its performance advantage was consequently small. Its maximum speed was only 290 mph and it operational ceiling 22,000 feet; range with a 14,000-pound bomb load was 2,250 miles, and with this kind of load, plus full fuel tanks, speed was reduced to 230 mph. Nevertheless, it was thought that Lincolns operating by night would add substantially to the weight of the air offensive against Japan, and the first Lincoln squadrons were earmarked for the Pacific Theatre, though the war was over before they were ready to leave the United Kingdom.

The English Electric Company had designed a jet bomber,

later to be known as the Canberra, but this would not fly in prototype form until May 1949 and it would be another two years before it began to replace the Lincoln in RAF service. Moreover, the twin-jet Canberra was a light bomber, with insufficient range to penetrate deeply into Soviet territory. An indication of the deficiency in Bomber Command's strategic delivery systems is the fact that, beginning in 1950, eighty-seven B-29s were loaned to the RAF to sustain its strategic capability until the first of the V-Bombers entered service. In RAF service the B-29 was named the Washington.

The Superfortress was far more advanced than the Lincoln in every respect except its bomb-carrying ability. In the late 1930s, whereas Britain's potential enemy was Germany — leading to a requirement for a bomber capable of delivering a heavy load over medium ranges — the biggest threat to American interests was the expansionism of Imperial Japan. Several US aircraft companies were therefore asked to submit design studies for a new and advanced bomber capable of carrying a substantial bomb load over great distances; in other words, one that would be able to strike at Japan from American bases in the Pacific.

The result was the B-29, the biggest, heaviest and most modern bomber of the Second World War. With a normal range of 3,250 miles — twice that of, say, the Avro Lancaster or Boeing's earlier B-17 Flying Fortress — a top speed of 357 mph at 30,000 feet and a bomb load of 12,000 pounds, this was the aircraft which, in 1944–45, brought the war to the Japanese home islands.

Production of the B-29 ended in May 1946, after 3,970 had been built, but subsequently modifications included SB-29 (search and rescue), TB-29 (trainer), WB-29 (weather reconnaissance) and KB-29 (flight refuelling tanker) variants. The KB-29M had the British-developed probe and drogue flight refuelling equipment, and the KB-29P used the Boeing flying boom method, which was standardised in the USAF. Two production variants, the B-29C and the B-29D, were cancelled at the end of the war, but the design of the B-29D underwent substantial changes to become the B-50, which began to re-equip Strategic Air Command squadrons in 1947.

Although retaining the general appearance and characteristics of the B-29, the B-50 was in fact seventy-five per cent new, with a new aluminium wing structure some sixteen per cent stronger, twenty-six per cent more efficient and several hundred pounds lighter than the B-29's. The vertical tail surfaces were five feet higher than those of the B-29 and were hinged to fold horizontally over the starboard tailplane to enable the new type to be housed in existing hangars. Having replaced the B-29 in SAC service, the B-50 remained the mainstay of America's strategic bombing force until the early 1950s, when it began to be replaced by a new generation of jet bombers.

The most widely used version, the B-50D, had a top speed of 400 mph at 25,000 feet, and could reach an altitude of 40,000 feet with a sizeable bomb load. Its range with a 10,000-pound bomb load — in other words, a single early-generation atomic weapon — was 6,000 miles, though it could lift up to 28,000 pounds of bombs over shorter distances. Carrying single atomic bombs and operating from bases in Alaska, B-50s flying over the North Pole could have hit targets in the eastern USSR.

The B-50 therefore filled an important gap, but it was little more than an interim development pending the arrival of more advanced aircraft. The first of these, and the first bomber with truly global strategic capability to serve with any air force, was the mighty Convair B-36, unofficially named the Peacemaker, originally conceived during the Second World War as a means of bombing Germany from bases in the United States. Half as big again as the B-29 and powered by six Pratt & Whitney R-4360 piston engines, the prototype B-36 flew in August 1946, and the first operational aircraft were delivered to Strategic Air Command two years later.

As relations between East and West froze into what was to become known as the Cold War, the B-36 became a very important weapon indeed in America's arsenal; with a range of 8,000 miles, it was capable of obliterating Moscow. Before the advent of the B-36, the B-29 and B-50 had been classed as heavy bombers; alongside the B-36, which weighed 160 tons fully loaded compared with the B-50's 80 tons, they were downgraded to the medium bomber category. Aircraft like the twin-engined B-26 Invader, which had previously been classed as medium bombers, consequently became light bombers.

In the summer of 1947, at the time of the USAF's formation, Strategic Air Command could look forward to even more exciting aircraft. The USA's first venture into the jet bomber field was the North American B-45 Tornado, which first flew in 1947 and entered production a year later; but this had a combat radius of only 500 miles and was essentially a tactical aircraft to replace such twin-engined types as the B-26 and the B-25 Mitchell. Although it could carry nuclear weapons, the B-45 had no strategic application.

This was far from true of another jet bomber project which had started life in September 1945 as the Boeing Model 450. In a radical departure from conventional design, this featured a thin, flexible swept wing based on wartime German research data and carried six turbojets in underwing pods. Basic design studies were completed in June 1946, and a prototype flew in December 1947. As the Boeing B-47 Stratojet, the bomber would eventually enter service with Strategic Air Command's medium bomber force in 1951. A second Boeing project, arising out of a USAF requirement for a new jet aircraft to equip Strategic Air Command's heavy bomber force, was to emerge in 1954 as the mighty B-52 Stratofortress — an aircraft that would continue to form the backbone of America's airborne nuclear deterrent thirty years later.

In developing their new generation of jet bombers, American designers had taken the bold step of leapfrogging existing technology — admittedly with the aid of a whole range of advanced German aerodynamic research — to produce a series of aircraft that would revolutionise the whole concept of air warfare. The same was true of fighter development, and in this respect too the deficiencies of British equipment — or rather the governmental indecision that resulted in the development of superb new British fighters being protracted almost beyond credibility — were to play a part in the eventual decision to station American combat units in Britain during the cold-war crises that were yet to come.

The main obstacle to military aircraft development in Britain in the early years of the jet age was that there was little attempt to centralise effort or pool knowledge, so that the work of British aircraft designers progressed along independent lines, often with a wasteful duplication of effort. This was a sad state of affairs, because Britain had ended the war at the forefront of jet aero-engine technology; but, as in the bomber field, her first-rate turbojets had been married to conventional airframe designs, the Gloster Meteor and the de Havilland Vampire being classic examples.

The Meteor had entered RAF service in the summer of 1944, in time to take part in the air defence of southern England against the German V-1 offensive, and the squadrons of Fighter Command had begun to equip with the Vampire in 1946. Yet these two aircraft, which by the end of the 1940s were totally outclassed by fighter types being produced in quantity in both the United States and the Soviet Union, were to form the mainstay of Fighter Command for the best part of a decade.

It was only in 1951, when events in Korea indicated that World War Three might be just around the corner, that a trio of new and advanced British fighters — the Hawker Hunter, Supermarine Swift and Gloster Javelin — were ordered into 'super-priority' production for the RAF. The Hunter and Swift did not enter squadron service until 1954 — even then the Swift proved a failure as a fighter — and it was another two years before the Javelin all-weather interceptor arrived; in the meantime, as we shall see, the Americans had stepped in and given the air defences of Great Britain a much-needed injection of modern fighter aircraft.

It was a British turbojet that had powered the prototype of the first jet fighter to go into quantity production for the USAF, the Lockheed F-80 Shooting Star. Early production F-80As entered USAF service late in 1945 with the 412th Fighter Group, which became the 1st Fighter Group in July 1946 and comprised the 27th, 71st and 94th Fighter Squadron, and for the next five years the F-80 was the workhorse of the USAF's tactical fighter-bomber and fighter interceptor squadrons.

The first of the new types designed to replace the F-80, flown as a prototype in February 1946, was the Republic F-84 Thunderjet, the first fighter-bomber capable of carrying a tactical atomic bomb and the type that ultimately provided many of

NATO's air forces with their first experience of jet combat aircraft. In its ultimate F-84G version the Thunderjet could carry a formidable load of rockets and bombs in addition to its built-in armament of six .5-inch machine guns; it also had a range of 2,000 miles at 480 mph cruising speed, and this could be greatly extended with the use of flight refuelling, making the Thunderjet very useful for rapid overseas deployment in times of tension. The F-84, however, was a conventional design lacking the performance of more advanced swept-wing fighters, which made it vulnerable in a hostile environment, and it was eventually replaced by a swept-wing derivative, the F-84F Thunderstreak.

The real star of post-war fighter development in the United States was the North American F-86 Sabre, without doubt one of the finest of all combat aircraft. The F-86 had its origin in a 1944 USAAF requirement for a medium-range day fighter; at that time North American were working on the design of a carrier-borne jet fighter, the FJ-1 Fury, and a version of this was offered to the USAAF, minus its naval equipment. Three prototypes were ordered in May 1945 under the designation XP-86.

Like its naval counterpart, the XP-86 had a straight wing, but with the availability of captured German aerodynamic research material it was decided to adopt swept flying surfaces, and this called for substantial redesign. The prototype swept-wing XP-86 flew in October 1947 and the first operational Sabre unit was the 94th Squadron of the 1st Fighter Wing, which equipped in January 1949. Two years later, over Korea, the Sabre was to give an outstanding account of itself in combat with Russian-built MiG-15s, destroying ten enemy fighters for every Sabre lost.

Such was the line-up of USAF combat aircraft, either in service or under development, at a time of growing international tension that was soon to explode into crisis. To appraise fully the causes of the tension, and the renewed involvement of American forces in Europe — specifically in England — during the late 1940s, it is necessary at this juncture to examine the military policies of the Soviet Union following the defeat of Germany and Japan.

The Soviet Union ended the Second World War with a completely different strategic concept from that of the United States. The Russians, at an appalling cost in lives and material, had been forced to sacrifice large areas of their homeland after the German invasion of June 1941 in order to buy time to organise their vast superiority in manpower and battlefield weapons. At the end of the war, therefore, the Russians lost no time in seizing the Baltic, eastern Europe and the Balkans, areas that were the historical jumping-off points for invasions of Russian territory, and — unlike the western powers — retained many of their forces in a state of readiness. The United States, on the other hand, had put its main effort during the war into acquiring control of the seas and in forging a powerful long-range air strike force, which was complemented at the end of the war by America's monopoly on nuclear weapons. As one strategic analyst put it:

> In short, the United States fought on a world-wide scale and developed the weapons and strategic concepts for such a war; the Soviet Union, to all intents and purposes, fought a local war using battering-ram tactics and did not develop the weapons and strategy that would enable her to reach the United States. It is not surprising that postwar Soviet spokesmen stressed Stalin's military science with its glorification of the infantry and artillery, and avoided mentioning the nuclear threat, or did so only in a derogatory manner. But in spite of this obeisance to artillery as the god of war, with air power as only one of the handmaidens, there must have been agonizing reappraisals under way in the Kremlin. The Russians were sitting under the United States Strategic Air Command's bombsights, and they were not happy.*

In fact, at any time during the two years immediately after the war, the Russians could have launched an invasion of western Europe and reached the English Channel in a matter of days. They alone of all the former Allied powers had armed

---

* K. R. Whiting in *The Soviet Air and Rocket Forces*, ed. Asher Lee (1976), Greenwood Press, New York (facsimile of 1959 edition).

forces that were still intact, and although the United States would certainly have used atomic weapons against them, only a limited stockpile of these as yet existed. The Americans could have hurt the Russians badly, but they could not have prevented the Red Army seizing its objectives in Europe. As things turned out, Stalin was far too preoccupied with his other recent gains to think of committing his forces to an offensive in the West; the newly-conquered satellites in eastern Europe and the Balkans needed to be brought under firm control; the situation in the Far East was still unstable; and there were political moves to be made in Greece, Turkey and Iran.

Even without nuclear weapons, the mighty Red Army provided Stalin with an ideal tool for tightening his stranglehold on eastern Europe; beyond that, until he possessed his own nuclear weapons and the means to deliver them, there was little he could do except use the Red Army within its capabilities while proclaiming that long-range bombers and atomic weapons were nothing more than paper tigers. He realised that only by dismissing those weapons in derogatory fashion, while simultaneously glorifying his own strength — large ground forces, supported by masses of armour and a powerful tactical air force — could he keep the morale of the Red Army and the Soviet people at an acceptable level. Even if he did not believe his own doctrine, he had little choice but to downgrade the American strategic threat until he had at least enough of his own strategic weapons to run a reasonable bluff. But Stalin, with justification, was probably convinced that the United States had neither the intention nor the resources to deliver a mortal blow against the Soviet Union. In the meantime, the Red Army was more than adequate for the purpose of consolidating post-war Soviet gains.

Behind the scenes, Stalin and his advisers were desperately trying to acquire the very weapon systems they were publicly decrying, and enormous amounts of scarce resources and even scarcer technical personnel were being poured into research and development. With the wartime emphasis on the development of tactical bombers, assault aircraft and fighters, Soviet designers had had little time to study long-range bomber projects, and it had become obvious that even if work on such projects had begun in 1944 there would still have been a serious delay before a Soviet long-range bomber could be manufactured in quantity.

The answer to the problem had, quite literally, dropped out of the Russian sky. During 1944 four USAAF B-29s made forced landings in Soviet territory, having sustained battle damage while attacking Japanese targets in Manchuria. Their crews were returned to the USA in due course but the Russians kept the bombers, and Stalin gave the prominent aircraft designer Andrei N. Tupolev the job of producing a perfect copy of the American aircraft; at the same time, A.D. Shvetsov was given the task of copying its Wright R-3350 radial engines.

By copying the B-29 in every detail, the Russians hoped to by-pass all the technological problems associated with the development of an aircraft of this type in one step. The work was not easy and big snags cropped up frequently, particularly in connection with electronically operated equipment such as the gun turrets. Nevertheless, construction of the prototype Russian B-29 — designated Tupolev Tu-4 — was begun in March 1945, and the first three prototypes were ready for flight testing by the beginning of 1947. These were publicly revealed on 1 May 1948 during the big Soviet air display at Tushino, near Moscow; by that time production of the Tu-4 was well under way and the first examples had been delivered to the Soviet Air Force.

Stalin now had a vehicle capable of attacking targets in the United States across the Pole, though such an attack would have involved flight refuelling — which the Russians were also working hard to perfect — and would have been a one-way mission. What he still lacked was the atomic bomb.

The Russians were not as backward in nuclear research during the pre-war period as the West imagined. One leading Russian nuclear physicist, Peter Kapitsa, had worked in Lord Rutherford's laboratory in Cambridge in the 1920s, while V.I. Vernadsky, who had spent some time in the Curie Radium Institution in Paris, stated as early as 1922 that atomic energy would revolutionise human life. In that year he also founded the State Radium Institute in Leningrad, and A.F. Ioffe began to develop nuclear research in Leningrad's Physical-Technical

School in the early 1930s. Some of the most brilliant Soviet nuclear research men, such as Landau, Sinnelnikov, Frankel and Kurchatov, began their work in the 1930s, and in 1937 the first cyclotron in Europe was built at the Radium Institute in Leningrad.

The advent of war stimulated American nuclear research, but it had exactly the opposite effect in the Soviet Union. With Russia's scientists assigned to more pressing tasks there was no question of any massive investment of funds or skilled manpower in a nuclear weapons research programme; in fact, it is doubtful whether the Soviet leaders realised the military potential of atomic power. Even later in the war, when the Russians were made aware of Anglo-American work on the atomic bomb project, they could not comprehend the awesome power that was about to be unleashed.

Nevertheless, late in 1944 the Soviet nuclear scientists were sent back to their laboratories and urged to come up with a comparable weapon as soon as possible. As history has recorded, their task was made a great deal easier by espionage, and the first Soviet nuclear reactor went into operation in 1947. Even so, Western experts still predicted with confidence that it would take the Russians ten or fifteen years to produce an operational atomic bomb.

The experts were wrong. In 1947 the Russians were only two years away from exploding their first atomic device, and designs of new jet bombers that were to carry the operational Soviet bomb were already on the drawing-board. In the meantime, Russia and the West were to become locked in a major trial of strength; one that would bring the might of the United States Air Force back to Britain to establish a presence that still remains today.

2

The Crisis Years, 1948–53

THE TRIAL OF strength began in earnest on 20 April 1948, when the Russian military governor in Berlin, Marshal Vassily Danilovich Sokolovsky, and his advisers walked out of the four-power Allied Control Council in what appeared to be a pre-planned move designed to precipitate a crisis among the allied powers responsible for the administration of the shattered German capital. During succeeding weeks the Russians embarked on a systematic campaign of harassment; on 1 April, for example, they stated that permits would be required for Allied troop movements to Berlin through the Soviet-occupied zone of Germany. To the Allied military commanders, it seemed that the Russians were on the verge of severing the road and rail links altogether.

One thing was clear: Berlin, or at least the sectors of the divided city held by the western Allies, could not be defended. General Lucius Clay, the Military Governor in Germany and commander of the US forces in Europe, had only 6,500 troops in the Berlin area, and they were outnumbered three to one by the Russians. Instructed by the US Joint Chiefs of Staff to avoid the use of force at all costs, Clay's preoccupation lay in finding an immediate means of supplying the garrison and the civilian population of the western sectors of Berlin should the road and rail links be cut. (Over 600 tons of vital supplies had already been lost when the Russians delayed Allied train movements on 1 April.)

To test the feasibility of forging an air supply link with Berlin, Clay ordered the 61st Troop Carrier Group at Rhein-Main Air Base, near Frankfurt, to begin flying in supplies, with effect from 2 April, aboard its twenty-five C-47 transport aircraft, each of which could carry up to three tons of cargo. This operation encountered no interference from the Russians, but on 5 April there was an indication of what might happen in the future when a Viking airliner of British European Airways, on a routine flight to Berlin, was buzzed by a Soviet Yak-3 fighter as it approached the capital in one of the recognised air corridors. The Russian fighter made one pass, turned to make another, and collided head-on with the airliner. Both aircraft crashed, the Russian being killed along with ten passengers and crew in the Viking.

The Russians appeared to hold all the cards in the air as well as on the ground. The commander of the United States Air Forces in Europe, Lieutenant General Curtis LeMay — who had taken over from USAF's first commander, Brigadier General John McBain, in October 1947 — had only eleven operationally effective combat groups with about 275 aircraft, mostly A-26 attack bombers and F-51 Mustang and F-47 Thunderbolt fighters. In the British zone, the RAF had a few squadrons of Mosquitos, Spitfires and Tempests, while in their zone the French were operating a mixture of American and British equipment. Against this, the Russians had a tactical air force of some 4,000 combat aircraft in their zone of occupation.

LeMay determined that if war did come he would do his best to meet it with the scant resources available. Desperately concerned to protect the vital supply line between the American Zone and Bremerhaven, which was vulnerable to a sudden Russian armoured thrust, his first step was to set up a defence in depth by organising a series of air bases well to the west of the Rhine in France and Belgium. The Chiefs of Staff of the French and Belgian Air Forces, Generals Charles Lecheres and Lucien Leboutte, readily agreed to this plan and made several of their airfields available for American air reinforcement. Quietly and by devious methods the bases were stockpiled with bombs, fuel and spare parts, and 200 USAF ground crew in civilian clothing were assigned to each base. By the end of April 1948 LeMay had a string of operational airfields at his disposal, awaiting only the aircraft that would fly in if the Russians made a warlike move. The move finally came on 23 June 1948 in an

announcement by the Russian-controlled ADN Press Agency
in Berlin:

> The Transport Division of the Soviet Military Admin-
> istration is compelled to halt all passenger and freight traffic
> to and from Berlin tomorrow at 0600 hours because of tech-
> nical difficulties. It is impossible to reroute traffic in the
> interest of maintaining rail services, since such measures
> would unfavourably affect the entire railway system in the
> Soviet Zone of Occupation. Water traffic will also be sus-
> pended . . . Coal shipments from the Soviet Zone are halted.
> The Soviet authorities have also ordered the central switch-
> ing stations to stop the supply of electric power from the
> Soviet Zone and Soviet Sector to the Western sectors. Short-
> age of coal to operate the plants and technical difficulties at
> the Czernowitcz Power Station are the reasons given . . .

Such was the message that announced to the world that the
Russians were implementing their plan to force the British,
Americans and French out of Berlin by severing the city's vital
arteries. Their decision was to set in motion the great eleven-
month supply operation known as the Berlin Airlift.

In the beginning, the resources available to implement such
an operation were woefully slender; the Americans had only
100 transport aircraft — all C-47s — in Europe at the time, and
not all of them were serviceable. To this fleet the Royal Air
Force could add perhaps 150, again mostly C-47s (or Dakotas,
as the RAF called them); the French contribution looked like
being negligible, at least in terms of equipment, for most of
France's small force of transport aircraft were tied up in Indo-
China. This meant that against Berlin's daily food requirement
of 13,500 tons, the USAF and RAF between them could probably manage 700 tons.

The situation was clearly intolerable, and one that prompted
US President Harry S. Truman's close advisers to exercise
caution when it came to talk about an Allied stand over Berlin.
Some of the US Army chiefs were cautious, too; among them
were Major General William Draper, Under Secretary of the
Army, and Lieutenant General Albert Wedemeyer, the Army

General Staff's Director of Plans and Operations, who arrived in London on 24 June after a hurried transatlantic flight to sound out the opinion of the British Government. Their surprise was considerable when Ernest Bevin, the Secretary of State for Foreign Affairs, informed them that Prime Minister Clement Attlee's Cabinet had voted not to sanction a withdrawal from Berlin, and that RAF transport aircraft were already flying in supplies. In fact only half a dozen Dakotas were involved and the Cabinet believed that the situation would be back to normal in a few days, once the Russians had made their gesture; but the British attitude did much to strengthen American resolve.

In Washington, the resolve of President Truman needed no strengthening; he was adamant that the Western Allies should remain in Berlin. All that remained was to find a way of keeping them there in the face of mounting Soviet pressure. Truman's instruction to James Forrestal, Secretary of Defense, Kenneth Royall, Secretary of the Army, and Robert Lovett, Under Secretary of State, at a meeting on 25 June was quite specific; all resources were to be channelled into forming a viable airlift organisation. General LeMay's shoestring air bridge would soon be a thing of the past.

Once the airlift had been established on a large scale, the Russians must be dissuaded from interfering with it. That could only be achieved by dispatching modern combat aircraft to Europe with the utmost priority, and that meant the B-29, which had the capability to hit the Russians hard. In fact, only a relatively small number of Strategic Air Command's B-29s were equipped for the carriage and release of nuclear weapons at that time, and in any case no agreement existed between the British and US governments for the basing of American nuclear weapons on British soil. But the Russians were presumed to be unaware of this, and the presence of even a small force of B-29s in Britain would, it was thought, have a considerable deterrent effect. Agreement had existed since 1946, though not on a formal basis, between the British Air Ministry and the USAF for the use of British air bases by conventionally armed American bombers in the event of a war threat in Europe; its implementation now was little more than a formality to which the Attlee government readily agreed.

On 25 June the first eight Dakotas of RAF Transport Command arrived at Wunsdorf to begin airlift operations, and the lift got under way in earnest the next day with thirty-two sorties by USAF C-47s from Wiesbaden carrying a total of eighty tons of supplies to Tempelhof air base in the American sector of Berlin. On 28 June thirty-five Douglas C-54 Skymasters — four-engined transports with three times the capacity of the C-47 — left their bases in the Caribbean, Hawaii and Alaska to join the operation; arriving on 30 June, they were flying within a matter of hours. Early in July RAF Sunderland flying boats and Avro York transports also joined the airlift, and by 20 July the 54 C-54s, 105 C-47s, 40 Yorks and 50 Dakotas involved were carrying a combined daily tonnage of 2,250 tons.

Meanwhile, on 16 July, a joint announcement had been made by the British Air Ministry and the US Air Force to the effect that two Boeing B-29 medium bomber groups, totalling sixty aircraft, were flying from the USA to bases in England 'for a short period of temporary duty'; that this movement was 'part of the normal long-range flight training programme instituted over a year ago by the US Strategic Air Command' to which these groups belonged; and that the squadrons would be based at Marham in Norfolk and Waddington in Lincolnshire under the operational control of General Curtis LeMay, Commanding General of USAFE. It was also announced that C-54 aircraft would be transporting maintenance men and supplies to the UK, that each B-29 would carry regular and spare crews, and that about 1,500 men would be involved in the training.

To support the B-29 groups on their periods of temporary duty in England the Americans needed a supply and maintenance depot. The site selected was Burtonwood, in Cheshire, which in 1942 had been the central repair depot for all American-built aircraft and engines used by the RAF and the USAAF units which had just arrived to join the air offensive against Germany. The repair and maintenance facilities had been greatly expanded during the war years, and when the war ended a skeleton USAAF staff had remained to look after existing stocks of American equipment. Further maintenance facilities were created at Burtonwood in January 1946 with the formation of the RAF's No. 276 Maintenance Unit.

Burtonwood's wartime workshops and installations were still intact, and it was logical to reactivate them. Consequently, in the summer of 1948, USAF technical personnel were moved into the base to prepare support facilities for Project Skincoat, as the SAC deployments were to be called.

On 17 July 1948 thirty B-29s of the 28th Bomb Group, the first to be deployed, flew into their British base — not, as it turned out, either Marham or Waddington, but Scampton, recently vacated by the Lancasters and Wellingtons of the Bomber Command Instrument Rating and Examining Flight. The next day thirty more B-29s of the 2nd Bomb Group arrived at Lakenheath in Suffolk, and on 8 August the 307th Bomb Group, comprising the 370th and 371st Bombardment Squadrons, brought its Superfortresses to Marham.

Meanwhile, in the third week of July the first reinforcements for General Curtis LeMay's air defences in Europe had arrived in the shape of sixteen Lockheed F-80 Shooting Stars of the 56th Fighter Group, commanded by Lieutenant-Colonel David Schilling. The first stage of their journey had taken them from Selfridge AFB in Michigan via Bangor, Maine, to Goose Bay, in Labrador; from Labrador they flew to Bluie West, in Greenland, in 1 hour 50 minutes, then to Reykjavik, Iceland, in 1 hour 45 minutes, and from Iceland to Stornoway, in Scotland, in 1 hour 40 minutes, a total transatlantic flight time of 5 hours 15 minutes. From Stornoway the F-80s flew to Odiham, in Hampshire, where they refuelled for the last leg of the flight to their base in Germany.

This was not the first transatlantic flight by jet aircraft; that had been completed eight days earlier, on 12 July, by six de Havilland Vampire F.3s of No. 54 Squadron, RAF, which had left Odiham to carry out a goodwill tour of Canada and the United States. They had followed the same route as the F-80s, though in the opposite direction, and it had taken them three hours longer, partly because of their lower cruising speed and partly because they encountered jet streams of up to 200 mph at their cruising altitude of 35,000 feet.

On 14 August seventy-five more Shooting Stars arrived in Britain. This time they came by sea aboard the aircraft carrier USS *Sicily*, which berthed in the Clyde, where they were offloaded and taken to Prestwick for overhaul before flying on. It was the first of many occasions on which Prestwick was to be used as a staging post for USAF jet aircraft destined for the combat groups in Europe.

On 25 August the US Air Force announced that the contingent at Burtonwood was to be expanded to 2,500 personnel under the command of Lieutenant-Colonel Walter Ott. This would make Burtonwood the principal USAF base in Britain, and it would be responsible not only for supporting the three B-29 groups — the latter under the command of Major General Leon Johnson — but also for providing facilities for the supply and maintenance of American aircraft engaged in the rapidly expanding Operation Vittles, the Berlin Airlift. A few days later it was revealed that the number of US military aircraft in Europe — including the B-29s and the transports involved in the airlift — had risen to 466, and that the number of USAF personnel had increased to 18,000. About 6,000 of these, it was stated, would be based in Britain before the end of the year.

At this time the principal maintenance depot for the USAF aircraft engaged in the Berlin Airlift was Oberpfaffenhofen, in the American Zone, where the necessary 200-hour inspections were carried out. But facilities at this depot were primitive; aircraft were washed down with a mixture of kerosene and water on open-air ramps because there was no adequate hangarage, and with winter approaching it was clear that this would quickly become unacceptable. Top priority was therefore given to the rapid expansion of the Burtonwood facilities with the help of experienced technicians from the big US Air Materiel Command centre at Tinker AFB, near Oklahoma City, who arrived in the somewhat cooler climes of Cheshire early in September and set about reactivating the wartime maintenance facilities. Gradually, they set up a three-quarter-mile-long assembly line on which eight aircraft a day could be cleaned by commercial-type vacuum cleaners and then hosed down with detergent.

The smooth operation of the USAF facility at Burtonwood during the months that followed was crucial to the airlift operation as a whole; it is no exaggeration to say that the airlift could not have succeeded without it. All USAFE C-47s were withdrawn from the airlift at the end of September and from then on Burtonwood handled only the big four-engined C-54 Skymasters, which needed some twenty man-hours of maintenance for every flying hour. Every C-54 engaged in the airlift underwent checks after every 50, 100 and 150 hours' flying, the 100-hour check involving a change of spark plugs and oil. These checks were carried out at the aircraft's home base, but for the 200-hour inspection it was flown to Burtonwood for a six-phase check involving washing and cleaning the aircraft; running up the engines; carrying out maintenance work on engines, pipes and ignition; servicing the electrical system, instruments, cables and rigging; and inspecting the hydraulics, wheels, brakes and tyres; finally, each C-54 was subjected to a rigorous preflight check and cleared for its return to operations. The RAF, it should be mentioned, had its own Transport Command Major Servicing Unit at Honington.

Meanwhile, the B-29 groups in Britain had been carrying out a systematic training programme designed to familiarise the crews with their European environment — although many had seen service here during the war years — and in carrying out simulated bombing attacks on targets around the United Kingdom and in western Europe.

The original three groups remained in England for ninety days of temporary duty (TDY), setting the pattern for other Strategic Air Command units that were to follow. At Scampton, the 28th Bomb Group's B-29s were replaced by those of the 301st Bomb Group. These departed in their turn on 15 January 1949, whereupon Scampton reverted to RAF use with the arrival of No. 230 Operational Conversion Unit's Lancasters and Lincolns. There was no subsequent American presence at Scampton except for a short period in 1952, when two B-17 Flying Fortresses and two Lockheed Constellations of a United States Navy detachment used the station for a few weeks, supported by the 3930th Air Base Squadron.

The other two airfields allocated to Strategic Air Command, Marham and Lakenheath, continued with TDY detachments; at Marham, for example, the 307th Bomb Group was replaced in November 1948 by the 97th Bomb Group, comprising the 340th and 371st Bombardment Squadrons. Only one other

SAC B-29-equipped unit, the 22nd Bomb Group (2nd, 19th and 408th Bombardment Squadrons) was destined to use Marham; subsequent TDY detachments all operated the more advanced B-50. These were the 509th Bomb Group (393rd and 715th Bombardment Squadrons), the 43rd Bomb Group (64th Bombardment Squadron) and the 2nd Bomb Group (20th Bombardment Squadron). In April 1950 a USAF B-29 mobile training unit assisted RAF Bomber Command to train RAF crews in operating the first of the B-29 Washingtons loaned to the Command (No. 35 Squadron was the first to equip with the type). From then on Marham was synonymous with the RAF's strategic deterrent force, although SAC ground personnel continued to be based there until 1965.

Meanwhile, another British airfield had been allocated for use by SAC. This was Sculthorpe, near Fakenham in Norfolk, which had been used by squadrons of the RAF's No. 100 (Countermeasures) Group during the war before being closed for modernisation in 1945. Its runways were lengthened and it was reopened in December 1948, being administered by the RAF on a Care and Maintenance basis until February 1949, when the 92nd Bomb Group arrived with its B-29s.

This was one of the most tense periods of the Berlin Airlift. In January and February 1949 the tonnage of supplies flown into the German capital surpassed all previous records, and the Russians — perhaps for the first time — realised that they had involved themselves in a dilemma from which there was no graceful retreat. They had not believed it possible for the Western Allies to mount an operation of this size, let alone sustain it in all kinds of weather, but once it was in full swing there was nothing they could do about it short of shooting down the Allied transport aircraft, which — since the Allies had legal access to Berlin via the three air corridors — would have constituted an act of war.

They could, however, do a lot to harass the airlift without resorting to force, and this was their policy during the early weeks of 1949, when British and US intelligence sources indicated that additional Soviet Air Force fighter and bomber units were arriving on airfields in the Russian Zone. Shortly afterwards the Russians began what seemed to be a large-scale air

The Douglas C-47 Dakota sustained the Berlin Airlift for several weeks in 1948 until the arrival of four-engined C-54 Skymasters with their bigger load-carrying capacity.

As an insurance against Soviet aggression during the period of the Berlin Airlift, the US Strategic Air Command despatched the first Groups of B-29 Superfortress bombers to Britain. These aircraft were not nuclear-capable; in fact, the entire US atomic weapons stockpile in 1948 comprised two bombs.

exercise; Allied transport crews flying along the corridors reported that the Russians appeared to be constructing air-to-ground firing ranges directly below their flight paths. Before long the Allied crews began to encounter increasing numbers of Soviet aircraft in the corridors, and incidents multiplied; the Soviet aircraft involved were mainly piston-engined Yak-3s, La-9s and Il-2s, and the tactics employed by their pilots were varied and often ingenious.

One of the Soviet pilots' favourite tactics was to fly at high speed along the corridors, either singly or in formation and usually in the opposite direction to the streams of transport aircraft, and make a fast head-on pass at a transport, pulling up sharply at the last minute. In the ten months from August 1948 to May 1949, American transport crews alone reported 77 buzzing incidents in the corridors by Soviet aircraft, together with another 96 incidents that were loosely described as close flying. The Americans also stated that Russian fighters fired bursts of cannon and machine-gun fire in the vicinity of transport aircraft on fourteen separate occasions, although no instance of a deliberate attack was recorded.

What the Russians called 'routine air-to-ground firing practices' were frightening enough, though seldom dangerous. The Soviet fighters would orbit over the corridors in the vicinity of one of their firing ranges, flying singly or in pairs at about 6,000 feet, above the main stream of traffic. They would then go into a shallow dive towards the range, passing immediately in front of the transport aircraft with their guns firing all the way down. American pilots also reported Soviet anti-aircraft fire in the corridors on 54 occasions, though the gunners were careful to place their shells well clear of the transport aircraft.

Searchlights were the most common nuisance; the corridors were lined with batteries of them and they made accurate night flying — which was absolutely essential in such a high traffic density — very tiring. The Russians also tried jamming the Allied radio frequencies, both by the use of primitive countermeasures equipment and by the simpler expedient of ordering their pilots to use the frequencies as much as possible, filling the already overcrowded ether with Russian chatter.

Some incidents brought the Allied air forces in Europe,

including the UK-based squadrons, to full alert. On 24 January, for example, a Dakota of RAF Transport Command crashed in the Russian Zone near Lübeck; the radio operator and seven German passengers were killed. It was not known for some time whether the aircraft had been deliberately shot down, or whether this was the beginning of a general Soviet offensive against the aircraft using the corridors, and in the meantime the Allied air forces stood ready for action. There was a similar alert when a second RAF Dakota came down in Russian territory in March.

If it had come to a shooting war in the early part of 1949 there is no doubt that the Allied tactical air forces in Europe could have given an excellent account of themselves. General LeMay's fighter groups were now almost fully equipped with F-80 Shooting Stars, while the fighter squadrons of the RAF's 2nd Tactical Air Force were rapidly re-equipping with Vampires. The Lincoln heavy bomber squadrons of RAF Bomber Command, together with SAC's British-based B-29 groups, could also have delivered a formidable weight of explosives on strategic targets in eastern Europe, and the American monopoly on nuclear weapons — even though such weapons were not present in Europe — prevented the Russians from embarking on full aggressive action. In May 1949 the Russians backed down and reopened the access routes to Berlin; the era of strategic deterrence had begun.

By mid-1949, however, the strategic picture had begun to change. Many units of the IA-PVO, the Soviet Air Defence Force, were now equipped with MiG-15 jet fighters, which rendered the first-line aircraft of the western Allies — F-80s, Vampires, Meteors, Lincolns and B-29s — obsolescent almost overnight. The vulnerability of the B-29s was to be demonstrated when they encountered MiGs over Korea.

The Berlin Airlift had hammered home to the western Allies the necessity of forming a closely-knit defensive organisation. On 6 July 1948 talks on the question of collective defence in the North Atlantic area had begun between the United States, Canada and the Brussels Treaty powers (Belgium, France, Luxembourg, the Netherlands and the United Kingdom). In December 1948 negotiations on the drafting of a North Atlantic

Treaty were opened, and in March 1949 Denmark, Iceland, Italy, Norway and Portugal were invited to participate. The North Atlantic Treaty was formally signed in Washington on 4 April, to come into force on 24 August 1949.

The urgent necessity for the formation of a North Atlantic Alliance was underlined in September, when the western Allies were profoundly shocked to learn that the Soviet Union — years ahead of the schedule predicted by western experts — had detonated a nuclear device. The Americans, working on the basis of their own experience, judged that it would be some time before the Russians could build up a stockpile of atomic weapons, and in any case they lacked the means to deliver them, but the threat for the future was all too apparent; by the early 1950s the nuclear monopoly of the United States would be a thing of the past.

Strategic Air Command deployments to the United Kingdom continued, and 22 August 1949 saw the arrival of the first B-50A Superfortresses when the 63rd Squadron of the 43rd Bomb Group brought its aircraft to Sculthorpe. These aircraft were equipped for flight refuelling and were accompanied by several KB-29M tanker aircraft, and one of them, serialled 46-010 and named Lucky Lady II, had made aviation history earlier in the year by making the first non-stop flight around the world. Taking off on 26 February from Carswell Air Force Base, Fort Worth, under the command of Captain James Gallagher, it had landed back at the same base 94 hours later on 2 March, having refuelled four times in flight and covered a distance of 23,452 miles at an average speed of 239 mph. A few days after the 63rd Squadron's arrival in England the 65th Squadron of the 43rd Group also deployed to Lakenheath with its B-50As and KB-29Ms.

Meanwhile, changes had taken place in the administration of the Strategic Air Command force in Britain. Originally, the B-29 deployments had come under the control of the Third Air Division (Provisional) with a headquarters at RAF Marham, but when it became obvious that the presence of the B-29s was to be more than temporary the 'provisional' was dropped and on 8 September 1948 the HQ was transferred to Bushy Park, near London. On 15 April 1949 it moved again, this time to

South Ruislip, near Bovingdon aerodrome, which could be used by communications and transport aircraft. The maintenance organisation at Burtonwood, which had now reached huge proportions and was designated the 59th Air Depot Wing, continued to support the SAC detachments.

The C-54 Skymasters which had supported the Berlin Airlift so ably were now giving way to a new generation of USAF transport aircraft, the first of which became regular visitors to the British airfields in the closing months of 1949. The Boeing C-97 Stratofreighter, distinguished by its deep double-hulled fuselage, was to become the USAF's most widely used four-engined transport aircraft of the 1950s, while the massive Douglas C-74 Globemaster I heralded a new generation of heavy-lift transport aircraft capable of carrying 200 fully-equipped troops or large quantities of freight over long distances. The C-74 was later developed into the C-124A Globemaster II, which remained the USAF's standard heavy lift transport until replaced by the turboprop-powered Douglas C-133A in the late 1950s.

The news that the Russians had detonated an atomic device, together with intelligence indications that they were developing a new range of jet and turboprop bombers, gave fresh impetus to plans for strengthening NATO's strategic air power in Europe. In addition to the conversion of eight Bomber Command squadrons to the B-29 pending the introduction of the Canberra planned for 1951–2, it was decided to increase Strategic Air Command's UK commitment by making four more air bases available to the USAF. The first of Britain's own four-jet medium bombers, the Vickers Valiant, would not be in service until at least 1955, assuming that the flight test programme went to plan (the first flight of the prototype Vickers Type 660 was tentatively scheduled for the spring of 1951), and even then the buildup of the RAF's projected V-Force of medium-range jet bombers would be relatively slow. In the meantime, there would be a critical strategic bomber gap which could only be filled by the United States Air Force.

The decision to provide the additional bases was reached without controversy by the British government, following strong recommendations by the Air Ministry and the Air Staff, and in April 1950 an 'Ambassadors Agreement' was signed by US Ambassador Lewis Douglas and Aidan Crawley, UK Under Secretary for Air, to cover the reconstruction plan for the bases. The four airfields selected were RAF Fairford, Greenham Common, Brize Norton and Upper Heyford, control of which was assumed by RAF Bomber Command on behalf of SAC early in June. USAF survey teams moved in immediately, and soon afterwards an Engineer Aviation Battalion, a Maintenance Company, an Ordnance Company, an Engineer Depot Company and a Base Support Company were assigned to each location to prepare it for operational SAC units.

The work had scarcely begun when East-West tensions reached a new flashpoint. On 25 June 1950, at the instigation of the Soviet Union, the North Korean army moved over the border into South Korea in an attempt to bring the whole peninsula under Communist control by force. United Nations forces on the one hand and Chinese Communist armies on the other were soon committed to the fighting, and the Korean War developed into a bloody stalemate that was to drag on for three years.

From the end of 1950 the Strategic Air Command units using Lakenheath and Sculthorpe operated the latest version of the Superfortress, the B-50D. The first examples arrived with the 93rd Bomb Group (Lakenheath) and the 97th Bomb Group (Sculthorpe); both were accompanied by KB29P tankers with boom-type flight refuelling equipment. Both Lakenheath and Sculthorpe were officially handed over to the United States Air Force in January 1951, although since they remained technically Air Ministry property they retained the RAF designation.

While the four newly assigned airfields were being made ready for use, two more RAF stations were allocated to SAC following the outbreak of the Korean War. The first of these was Mildenhall, in Suffolk, which had been vacated by RAF Bomber Command in March 1949, and at the end of June 1950 an army of US engineers descended on the site, building a ring of anti-aircraft emplacements and a high security fence. In July the B-50As of the 329th Bombardment Squadron, 93rd Bomb

Group, arrived, and their period of temporary duty was prolonged until February 1951 by the international situation. They were replaced immediately by the B-50Ds of the 509th Bomb Group; in May 1951 this was replaced by the 2nd BG, which in its turn relinquished Mildenhall to the 22nd Bomb Group at the end of its 90-day TDY. The 509th, incidentally, was the unit that had been specially formed in September 1944 with selected crews for operational training in connection with a most secret weapons project: the dropping of the atomic bombs on Japan.

The second RAF airfield allocated to the USAF in August 1950 was Bassingbourn, in Cambridgeshire. In April 1944 the first B-29 to visit Britain had landed there; now, a little over six years later, the 353rd Bombardment Squadron of the 301st Bomb Group, which had been controlling them, moved its HQ elsewhere, leaving the airfield to be used exclusively by the Americans. The 353rd BS stayed until January 1951, when it was replaced by the 38th Squadron, 55th Strategic Reconnaissance Wing, whose RB-50Bs undertook electronic and photographic surveillance missions over the Baltic and off northern Russia until May, when the 97th Bomb Group moved in with B-50Ds. The 97th remained at Bassingbourn until September 1951, when the station reverted to RAF use.

The other important development of 1950 took place at Manston, in Kent. Close to the English Channel and consequently to the continent, Manston was an important wartime fighter airfield and had been used subsequently by RAF Transport Command as a staging post for flights overseas. In July 1950 it was decided to transfer Manston to American use, although the station would remain under RAF control as part of No.11 Group, Fighter Command. Before the end of July the airfield had been occupied by the 7512th Air Base Group, and a few days later the 20th Fighter-Bomber Wing arrived with its Republic F-84E Thunderjets. Their task was to provide fighter escort for the B-50s should the latter have to be used in a tactical role over a European battlefield.

The 20th FBW was not specifically designated for this role and its presence at Manston was essentially a stop-gap measure pending the arrival of the 31st Fighter Escort Wing, also with

F-84Es, in January 1951; the 31st was replaced in turn by the 12th FEW in June. To provide search and rescue facilities a detachment of SA-16 Albatross and SB-29 Superfortress aircraft of the 9th Air Rescue Squadron was deployed to Manston in April 1951.

To demonstrate to their European allies that Strategic Air Command now had a truly global capability, the Americans sent detachments of massive Convair B-36 bombers to Lakenheath and Sculthorpe early in 1951; seven aircraft came to the former base, accompanied by C-124 Globemaster II transports carrying spares and ground crews. The bombers were of the B-36D variant, having four General Electric J47 turbojets paired in pods under the outer wings to supplement the six piston engines and provide additional power for increased speed over the target area; snap-action bomb doors replaced the sliding type used in earlier models; and they carried a formidable defensive armament of twelve 20-mm cannon in six remotely controlled retractable turrets, plus a 37-mm cannon in the nose. During their stay in Britain the B-36s flew a number of training sorties and practised fighter affiliation exercises with RAF Fighter Command, dwarfing the Meteors and Vampires that came up to intercept them.

Behind the scenes, Strategic Air Command was seriously concerned about the growing vulnerability of aircraft like the B-36. Korea, where the B-29 squadrons had suffered a fearful mauling at the hands of Chinese MiG-15s before being restricted to night operations, had shown that even bombers with the B-36's formidable power were unlikely to survive long in an environment dominated by enemy jet fighters. By the end of 1950, too, the Russians had the ingredients of an effective air defence system comprising radar, anti-aircraft guns and interceptors, all of which were being evaluated under operational conditions in Korea.

The problem would not be solved until Strategic Air Command was fully equipped with a new generation of advanced jet bombers such as the Boeing B-47 Stratojet, the first of which was scheduled to enter service later in 1951. In the meantime, as a result of the lessons of Korea, the USAF had resurrected the long-range escort fighter concept. Early thoughts on this, in

1948, had revolved around the idea of the B-36 carrying its own escort fighter, and to that end the McDonnell Aircraft Company had designed the diminutive XF-85 Goblin, which could be carried in a B-36's bomb bay, launched and then retrieved in flight. Tests had proved unsuccessful, however, and the scheme had been dropped.

As early as 1946, McDonnell had begun detailed design work on a heavy, long-range jet fighter designated XF-88, and the construction of two prototypes had been started in 1947 under a USAF contract. The first of these, powered by two Westinghouse XJ34 turbojets mounted side by side in the fuselage, flew in October 1948, but its range and altitude performance left a lot to be desired and the development programme was abandoned in August 1950, when the USAF shelved its long-range heavy fighter plans.

In 1951, with the concept alive once more, McDonnell revised the XF-88 design to produce a completely new aircraft, lengthening the fuselage to accommodate two powerful Pratt & Whitney J57 turbojets — engines that gave the new fighter a top speed of over 1,000 mph and a ceiling of 52,000 feet — and additional fuel. In its new guise, as the F-101A Voodoo, it was to serve the USAF well for many years in the tactical support and reconnaissance roles, even after the penetration fighter requirement was cancelled once more, and was to become a familiar sight in British skies.

As part of the programme to strengthen the defences of western Europe, a new agreement was signed in the spring of 1951 between the British and United States governments covering a special airfield construction programme designed to provide a total of thirty bases in the United Kingdom from which both strategic and tactical USAF air operations could be conducted. To control these expanding activities the Third Air Division was replaced on 1 May 1951 by the Third Air Force, with its headquarters at South Ruislip. It was to be under the control of USAFE and commanded by Major-General Leon W. Johnson, who had commanded the Third Air Division in Britain since 1948.

The upgrading of the USAF's commitment in the United Kingdom to the status of an Air Force brought more changes, particularly in the concept of USAF air operations in Britain: so far, the emphasis had been exclusively on a strategic operation, but a tactical mission was now added. To attend to the continued Strategic Air Command detachments on rotational duty in the UK, HQ Seventh Air Division was formed at South Ruislip under the command of Major-General Archie J. Old, and preparations were made for the Third Air Force to receive tactical units to support its new mission. It was also to be responsible for the logistical support of the USAF and other US units in Britain, and to seal the foundations of the new structure a Joint Transfer Agreement, delineating the responsibilities of the two Commands, was signed on 16 May 1951.

One of the first consequences of the new organisation was that Prestwick was reactivated to provide support for the increased volume of Military Air Transport Service aircraft now plying between the United States and Britain, and also to provide air-sea rescue coverage of the eastern Atlantic. A big new hard standing area was built, the main runway was extended, and the adjacent airfield of Ayr, which had been closed since 1946, was reopened as a USAF storage site. On 31 July 1951 two Sikorsky H-19 search and rescue helicopters landed at Prestwick after completing the first crossing of the Atlantic by rotorcraft; they had been escorted by a C-47 and a Grumman Albatross.

August 1951 saw the arrival in Britain of the first North American F-86A Sabres, at that time the most advanced day fighters in service anywhere in the world. The first F-86As had been rushed into action in Korea to counter the MiG-15s and had succeeded in establishing a considerable measure of air superiority over the disputed Yalu River; now they had arrived in England to give a much-needed boost to the effectiveness of Britain's air defences. The Sabres belonged to the 81st Fighter Interceptor Group, whose 116th Squadron touched down at Shepherd's Grove in Suffolk — one of the airfields loaned to the USAF under the terms of the new agreement — on 27 August 1951. It was joined there shortly afterwards by the 92nd Squadron, while the 91st Squadron arrived at nearby Bentwaters on 3 September. This was the first time that foreign aircraft had been assigned to the air defence of Great Britain.

There was another first in November 1951, when the 123rd Fighter-Bomber Wing of the Kentucky Air National Guard arrived at Manston with its F-84Es to replace SAC's 12th Fighter Escort Wing and become the first ANG unit to be deployed to Britain, the part-time personnel having been mobilised as a result of the Korean War. Air National Guard personnel were rotated to Manston until July 1952, when the 123rd FBW was deactivated and its aircraft used to form the 406th Fighter-Bomber Wing, which comprised the 512th, 513th and 514th Fighter Bomber Squadrons. The 406th used Thunderjets until November 1953, when it received Sabres and the new designation Fighter Interceptor Wing. Also in 1952, the air-sea rescue detachment at Manston was upgraded to squadron status, becoming the 66th Air Rescue Squadron.

The strength of the Third Air Force continued to expand rapidly, in terms of both equipment and personnel, until by June 1952 the South Ruislip HQ controlled an Air Division, a Light Tactical Bomb Wing, and three tactical Fighter Wings. The Air Division was the 49th, of which the 20th Fighter Bomber Wing and the 47th Bombardment Wing were the component parts. The 20th FBW arrived in June 1952, having flown its F-84G Thunderjets via Labrador and Iceland; two of its squadrons, the 55th and 77th, went to Wethersfield in Essex, while a third, the 79th, was based at Woodbridge.

The 20th FBW had a flight refuelling capability and its tanker aircraft were based at Sculthorpe base for the other component of the 49th Air Division, the 47th Bombardment Wing, whose two squadrons — the 84th and 85th — arrived on 31 May 1952 with their four-jet North American B-45 Tornados. Later, in March 1954, the 86th Squadron was added to the 47th BW's strength, giving it a total complement of 75 aircraft. The arrival of these units, with their associated supporting organisations, brought the number of USAF personnel in Britain to more than 45,000 by the autumn of 1952.

Meanwhile, the number of British bases available to Strategic Air Command had also increased. By the closing weeks of 1951 Upper Heyford's main runway had been lengthened to 10,000 feet and most of the planned expansion had been completed (under the control of the 7509th Air Base Squadron), permitting the arrival of the KB-29P tankers of the 93rd Air Refuelling Squadron from Castle Air Force Base, California, early in December to begin their ninety-day period of temporary duty. Upper Heyford saw further construction work during 1952 and the airfield defences were substantially strengthened; during the year the Oxfordshire base was host to KB-29P tankers that served the 97th, 509th and 2nd Bombardment Groups, as well as the KB-29Ms responsible for flight refuelling the 301st Bombardment Group.

Greenham Common, which was to be the subject of much controversy in later years, was formally handed over to the Strategic Air Command's Seventh Air Division on 18 June 1951, and US engineers set about the systematic destruction of the airfield's wartime hangars and buildings to make room for a new 10,000-foot runway, together with taxiways and hard standings. Not only the former airfield buildings were destroyed: forty-four local families had to be rehoused when their homes became the victims of a government compulsory purchase order, and two local pubs were bulldozed. Such was the scale of the reconstruction work at Greenham that the airfield would not be ready for use by SAC until the autumn of 1953.

Work on a lesser scale also went ahead at the Oxfordshire airfield of Brize Norton, and the first SAC deployment to this base took place in the last days of June 1952, when twenty-one B-36D and B-36F bombers of the 11th Bombardment Wing arrived from Carswell Air Force Base in Texas. Other SAC units to visit Brize Norton in 1952 were the 43rd and 301st Bombardment Wings, with B-50As.

The big increase in US personnel stationed in Britain during the early 1950s may not have been welcomed by the people who lived in the vicinity of the major air bases, but the good-time girls and petty racketeers were having a field day. One rather comical story that emerged in January 1953 concerned a hoaxer who, wearing a USAF officer's uniform, made a habit of touring bars in London's West End and warning the publicans that they must either ban unaccompanied women from their establishments or face losing American custom. His method was to draw landlords aside for a confidential chat, which was invariably accompanied by a large drink at the landlord's expense, and in the course of which he warned that the US command in Britain frowned on what he described as the 'female sharks' who were only interested in the GIs' fat wallets.

Publicans all over the West End spent several nights throwing prostitutes off their premises until the US Air Force felt compelled to come up with an official denial. 'The man is an imposter,' said a USAF spokesman. 'We would not dare send officers into London to tell publicans or anyone else how to run their businesses. We have had a number of phone calls concerning this man's activities during the past few weeks and believe someone is out to stir up trouble between Americans and the civilian population.'

Whoever the joker was, he was never caught, and somewhere in the South of England a middle-aged gentleman probably still enjoys a quiet chuckle over the brief furore he created. Nevertheless, in other areas prostitution near US bases was giving serious cause for concern, as the *Sunday Pictorial* reported in May 1953.

Good-time girls who have been spending profitable weekends in seaside towns near an American air base are worried. Recently they have been getting the cold shoulder instead of pound notes from American airmen in Margate, Ramsgate and Broadstairs. One girl, who has been a regular weekender throughout the winter, said yesterday: 'It's not worth going to Margate now. Last week I didn't go out with any Americans.' The man who has done most to stamp out the camp followers' racket is Colonel J. Herlick, in charge of the US base at Manston. He makes his men attend lectures on the perils of mixing with good-time girls and he has banned 'undesirables' from camp dances. Southampton is now the Mecca for good-time girls. They have found the pickings are easier there at the transit camp.

A spiralling traffic in the illegal sale of duty-free goods forced the USAF to impose strict security controls early in 1953, when spot checks revealed that carloads of contraband — sometimes even the cars themselves — were being smuggled out of US air bases for sale to racketeers. Despite the controls, the problem, like that of prostitution, was never satisfactorily resolved.

On a more serious note, the residents of Mablethorpe in Lincolnshire had a serious fright when a practice bomb fell off an F-84 Thunderjet after becoming hung up during a run over a practice bombing range in the sand dunes about five miles outside the town. The 25-pound explosive-filled missile smashed through three inches of concrete into the back yard of the biggest draper's store in town, only yards away from shoppers in the high street. Fourteen-year-old Brenda Hewson, a Girl Guide, was passing within ten yards when the bomb exploded, but a six-foot high solid wooden gate protected her. 'I heard a whistling and then an explosion,' she said, 'there was a huge cloud of smoke and bits of concrete came flying over the gate.' The bomb made a crater two feet deep, but luckily no-one was hurt. The incident was compounded by the fact that only 24 hours earlier a sand-filled practice bomb had fallen off an RAF jet after a similar hang-up and narrowly missed some bathers.

Inevitably, the increased tempo of air operations arising from the USAF buildup in the United Kingdom brought about a rise in air accidents, and consequent civilian fears of a catastrophe. Unlike the RAF, the Americans seemed to have few qualms about flying over densely populated areas at all altitudes. For example, there was an outcry following an incident on 7 February 1953, when a B-36 — one of seventeen making a dawn arrival at Fairford after flying from Carswell — got into difficulties in the airfield circuit. The captain, Lieutenant-Colonel Herman Gerick, ordered his crew of fifteen to bale out, which they did successfully. The problem was that the massive bomber flew on for thirty miles with nobody on board before crashing near the village of Laycock, fortunately without hurting anyone.

The growing American presence brought an increase in the number of British civilian employees at the US air bases; perhaps predictably, there was soon a degree of conflict between the Americans, who were used to getting things done, and the Trade Unions, who apparently were not. In one incident, in May 1953, a British woman civil servant, Mrs Nancy

Buckley, had her fingerprints and photograph taken for USAF records while she was working at Burtonwood, which was an entirely routine procedure. However, it brought an official protest from her union, the Civil Service Clerical Association, and a subsequent promise from the USAF that such a thing would not happen again.

A few months later it was the turn of the Constructional Engineering Union, which stepped in when two workmen, sacked because they objected to working conditions at Fairford, alleged that they had been removed from the base at gunpoint. The two men, Michael Kelly and F.McHale, refused to leave the camp until a union official arrived to hear their complaints; neither had been employed for a month — the statutory time for giving notice — and so the foreman dismissed them at once. They asserted that a USAF vehicle had driven up and that they had been forced to get into it at gunpoint before being escorted from the base. In this case the union didn't have a leg to stand on, and knew it, and the matter was quietly dropped.

Growing rumours that the Americans were stockpiling atomic weapons at their British bases in 1953 caused a lot of concern which, in fact, was unfounded. When the USAF returned to Britain in 1948 the entire American nuclear arsenal consisted of two 20-kiloton weapons; following the Berlin blockade President Truman had ordered a crash programme to produce more, and this had been continued when President Eisenhower took office in 1952. By that time bombs were being produced at the rate of one a day, so that by early 1953 the stockpile had risen to about 1,500. The majority of these were what would nowadays be described as tactical weapons, with a yield of between 20 and 40 kilotons, but collectively they represented an awesome destructive power. Since the Soviet Union had yet to deploy operational atomic weapons, there was no necessity to deploy US weapons of this kind at advanced overseas bases for the time being, although the facilities for storing them existed with the creation of secure weapons dumps at places like Fairford and Upper Heyford.

Nevertheless, the possibility that the USAF might deploy even a small number of atomic weapons to Britain, with the consequent possibility that the Soviet Union — assuming she had bombs of her own — might subject Britain to a first strike in order to eliminate advanced SAC bases in time of war, caused concern to Winston Churchill when he again assumed the office of Prime Minister in 1951, and in January 1952 he obtained an American assurance that atomic bombs would not be used from UK bases without the consent of the British government.

In fact, under Eisenhower's administration the United States government gave active encouragement to the development of Britain's own nuclear deterrent force. Such a force would act in concert with Strategic Air Command in time of war, and its deployment would relieve the USAF of a considerable strategic burden. Since 1946, when the McMahon Act had forbidden the disclosure of US nuclear information to other states, work on Britain's own bomb had been purely indigenous in nature, but despite the resulting delays and duplications the development of an operational British nuclear bomb had proceeded much faster than that of the aircraft that were to carry it. The first British atomic device — not yet a bomb — was successfully tested at Monte Bello in the Pacific on 3 October 1952, and the design of an aerodynamically suitable casing and an operational warhead went ahead during the winter of 1952–3.

Following a series of dropping trials with inert bomb shapes, the assembly of Britain's first operational nuclear weapon, code-named Blue Danube, continued throughout the summer of 1953. A 24-foot, 10,000-pound plutonium weapon, it had a warhead producing a yield of about 40 kilotons and was tested in its operational configuration at Woomera, Australia, on 14 October 1953,but it was to be another three years before an air drop was carried out. When RAF Bomber Command began to stockpile the component parts of its first Blue Danubes at Wittering in November 1953 the delivery of the Vickers Valiant that was to carry them was still eighteen months away, and by the time they arrived Blue Danube was already obsolescent. Ironically, after Eisenhower's initiative led to the renewed exchange of nuclear information between the United States and Britain, it was a much more refined generation of American nuclear weapons that was to equip the RAF's V-Force for much of its active life.

On the international chessboard, science was rapidly over-hauling political manoeuvring. On 6 November 1952 the United States exploded the first hydrogen device at Eniwetok Atoll in the Pacific, and in August 1953 the Russians, having progressed from the atomic stage with astonishing speed, also exploded a hydrogen bomb. The Cold War was beginning to escalate.

3

New Weapons, New Tasks

THERE WAS NO slackening in the tension between East and West during the early months of 1953. On 10 March two Czechoslovakian MiG-15s attacked a pair of USAF F-84 Thunderjets near Regensburg, inside Federal German territory, shooting one of them down; the pilot, Lieutenant W.G. Brown, baled out safely. Two days later a Lincoln of RAF Bomber Command, on a routine training sortie, strayed into the Soviet Zone as a result of a navigational error and was also shot down this time with the loss of its crew.

It was clearly time for further demonstration of USAF strength, and on 7 April two Boeing B-47 Stratojets landed at Fairford after a transatlantic proving flight of 5 hours 21 minutes. A little under two months later, on 2 June 1953, forty-five B-47s of the 306th Bomb Wing, comprising the 367th, 368th and 369th Bombardment Squadrons, arrived at Fairford after a formation flight across the Atlantic to position for a ninety-day rotational tour of duty.

The arrival of the B-47s signalled the beginning of the end for Strategic Air Command's piston-engined bomber fleet. With a top speed of over 600 mph the Stratojet was faster than many jet fighters then in service on either side, and the decision to go ahead with its production — taken at a time when most of the USAF's slender budget was committed to the procurement of the Convair B-36 — was to be amply vindicated. At the beginning of 1953 there were only sixty-two B-47s in SAC service, but by the end of the year the total had risen to 329, slightly outnumbering the B-36 fleet.

The service debut of the Stratojet, together with the growing arsenal of atomic weapons, finally gave Strategic Air Command the power of swift nuclear riposte; yet for anyone who saw the arrival of those early B-47s in Britain it was hard to believe that an aircraft of such striking beauty could carry in its belly the means to wipe out cities and cause death and destruction on an appalling scale.

The B-47's outstanding feature was its extremely thin wing, swept at an angle of thirty-five degrees and designed to give trouble-free handling at high subsonic speeds. The six General Electric J47 turbojets were mounted in underwing pods, so that in the event of an engine fire only the pod would suffer while the wing structure remained untouched. To boost the bomber's take-off performance at heavy loads — it could carry up to 20,000 pounds of bombs and weighed ninety tons fully loaded — it was fitted with eighteen solid-fuel rocket-assisted takeoff (RATO) bottles, nine on each side of the fuselage, giving an extra 18,000 pounds of thrust if required.

Although graceful in its true element, the Stratojet appeared ungainly on the ground because of its novel undercarriage arrangement, which consisted of two pairs of main wheels mounted in tandem under the fuselage and outrigger wheels under each wing; the main gear folded up into the fuselage, while the outriggers retracted into the inboard engine nacelles. The arrangement was light and space-saving but gave the B-47 a tendency to roll on takeoff, so that in a strong crosswind the pilot had to hold the control column right over to one side. Steering on the ground was accomplished by the nosewheel, which was adjusted to prevent the aircraft swinging more than six degrees either way. However, the aircraft's optimum attitude for takeoff was the one it assumed as it sat on the ground, and at about 140 knots, depending on its weight, the Stratojet literally flew itself off the runway with no need for backward pressure on the control column.

To pilots used to flying the B-29, B-50 or B-36, the main impression was of the Stratojet's speed, acceleration and rate of climb, all of which were colossal for its day. The bomber had fighter-like handling qualities and the cockpit layout resembled a fighter's too, with the pilot and co-pilot seated in tandem under a long, narrow canopy that gave excellent all-round visibility. The third crew member, the navigator, sat in the nose compartment and was also responsible for handling weapons release. The relatively small size of the pressurised crew compartment, and the fact that only three crew were carried instead of the twelve or thirteen in the previous generation of bombers, made the Stratojet a much more manageable aircraft, although the workload was correspondingly higher; for example, the co-pilot was responsible for handling the electrical and flight engineering equipment, operating the two remotely controlled radar-directed 20-mm cannon in the tail, and performing certain navigational functions such as taking star shots.

The need for all the runway reconstruction work at SAC's British bases was now apparent, for the Stratojet — even with RATO boosters — needed a very long take-off roll. Once off the ground, with flaps up and the aircraft automatically trimmed, the technique was to hold it down until safe flying speed had been reached and then climb at a shallow rate until 310 knots showed on the airspeed indicator, after which the rate of climb was increased to 4,000 or 5,000 feet per minute, depending on the aircraft's configuration.

At its operating altitude of 40,000 feet or more the B-47 handled lightly and could easily be trimmed to fly hands off. The quietness of the cockpit, the lack of vibration and the smoothness of the flight were noticeable, the only exception being when turbulence was encountered at high altitude in jet streams (the high-speed air currents that cut through the stratosphere). Then, looking out of the cockpit, the crew could see the B-47's long, flexible wings bending up and down — a rather unnerving phenomenon when experienced for the first time.

The B-47's maximum range was just over 3,000 miles, but this could be greatly extended by flight refuelling. On 4 August 1953, for example, a 306th BW B-47 flew from Fairford to McDill AFB in Florida, a distance of 4,450 miles, in nine hours 53 minutes, refuelling from a KB-29 tanker, and on 1 September Strategic Air Command took a big step towards a more effective flight refuelling system when a B-47 refuelled from a KB-47B Stratojet, demonstrating the practicality of jet aircraft topping up each other. It would be some time, however, before SAC received jet tankers in the form of the KC-135 variant of the Boeing 707 airliner; in the meantime the flight refuelling task devolved on the KC-97 Stratocruiser derivative, which gradually supplanted the KB-29 and the KB-50.

The B-47 had a spectacular landing technique that began with a long, straight-in approach from high altitude when the pilot dropped his undercarriage to act as an air brake; with landing gear down the Stratojet was capable of losing 20,000 feet in four minutes. Flaps were not lowered until final approach, which started several miles from the end of the runway and required great concentration. The bomber must not be allowed to stall, yet its speed had to be kept as low as was safely possible to prevent it running off the end of the runway. Each additional knot above the crucial landing speed added another 500 feet to the landing run, so the pilot had to fly to an accuracy of within two knots of the landing speed, which was usually about 130 knots for a light B-47 at the end of its sortie.

Ideally, the Stratojet pilot aimed to touch down on both tandem mainwheel units together, because if one or the other made contact with the runway first the aircraft bounced back into the air. With the wheels firmly down the pilot used his ailerons to keep the wings level, much as a glider pilot does after touchdown, and as the ailerons were moved the flaps automatically adjusted their position to help counteract roll; rudder had to be used very cautiously and sparingly or the aircraft might turn over. To slow the fast-rolling B-47 a brake parachute was deployed immediately on touchdown, and the pilot applied heavy braking. In addition, the aircraft was fitted with an anti-skid device which automatically released the brakes and then reapplied them to give fresh 'bite'. On average, the B-47's landing roll used up 7,000 feet of runway.

Early in September 1953, following the departure of the 306th BW, the 305th BW (medium) deployed a squadron of B-47's to Fairford and two other squadrons to Brize Norton. By this time B-47 detachments were also using Lakenheath and Upper Heyford; construction work at Greenham Common had been completed but the airfield would not be declared operational until the spring of 1954.

In September 1953 a new agreement, consolidating all previous agreements about the US commitment in Britain, was signed between the British and United States governments. It provided for the expansion of US base facilities in the United Kingdom — including non-flying stations — to a total of forty-three, with the cost of their establishment to be shared; nineteen of the bases were to house operational USAF units. The story finally broke in the UK press on 1 February 1954 as the result of the publication of the US House of Representatives sub-committee report, and at first there was only limited reaction to the news.

'US Air Bases in Britain — Burden of Cost Eased', *The Times* stated mildly, before continuing:

A House of Representatives sub-committee report of January 8, made public tonight (31 Jan) showed that the United States would provide $276m (£98m) in cash and $22m (nearly £8m) worth of military labour, Britain would provide $63m (£22m) in cash, $209m (more than £74m) worth of facilities, plus the land, and the use of a 400-mile pipeline built during the war at a cost of about $80 (£28m). Most of the bases are for medium bombers. Fifteen of the 19 are now ready for use.

Brigadier-General Stanley Wray, deputy director of United States Air Force installations, referring to the smaller amount of cash being provided by Britain, said the new agreement 'confirmed our impression that the economics of the United Kingdom would not permit the 50-50 cost sharing to proceed completely through the whole programme'.

General Wray said that only the bases at Elvington, Stansted, Chelveston and Bruntingthorpe were not in working condition. 'On the rest, I think, you could do operations now. You could not run full blast, but you could do operations if you were required to go'. Among the items to be added were American-style central heating systems. General Wray said: 'The British did not use a heating plant in our sense of the word. They used very ineffective little coal stoves. We found our respiratory infection rate and our disease rate pretty high under that system of heating.'

The continuing presence of the US bases in Britain, and their expansion, enjoyed the support of the majority of the Parliamentary Labour Party, as was revealed in the House of Commons on 9 February when Sir Winston Churchill replied to a question from Mr Tom Driberg (Lab., Maldon), who wanted to know whether the Americans were now regarded as a permanent feature. Bases for the US Air Force, the Prime Minister replied, would be provided in Britain for as long as necessary in the cause of world peace and security.

His declaration won immediate support from the Labour Front Bench; both Emmanuel Shinwell, former Defence Minister, and Arthur Henderson, former Secretary for Air, rounded sharply on Labour backbenchers who had questioned the financial and security dangers of the bases. 'We are not prepared to run away from our policy,' Mr Shinwell declared. 'In case there should be any misunderstanding, I am declaring the present policy of the Parliamentary Labour Party.'

Nevertheless, the subject of the US bases remained one of frequent debate during the early months of 1954. On 23 March Sir Winston Churchill, replying to questions about arrangements for consultation between Her Majesty's Government and the United States Government regarding the use of the United States' retaliatory air power in the event of a hostile attack on an ally of the United States in circumstances which might involve Britain in war, said:

So far as concerns the bases used by the Americans in this country, I would remind Hon. members of the communiqué agreed with the United States Government and issued on January 9, 1952, when the Foreign Secretary and I visited Washington: 'Under arrangements made for the common defence, the United States has the use of certain bases in the United Kingdom.' We reaffirm the understanding — that was the one arrived at by the Leader of the Opposition — 'that the use of these bases in an emergency would be a matter for joint decision by Her Majesty's Government and the United States Government in the light of circumstances prevailing at the time.' Mr Dulles' recent statements have been in full accord with this understanding.

The Prime Minister went on to speak of the frequent inter-changes on the subject which had taken place between himself and President Eisenhower. After a few more questions, none of which were of a searching nature, he concluded: 'It is remark-able, the restraint with which the Press have treated these matters. I only hope and trust that the nation and the thinking people in it will not in any way under-rate the overwhelming consequences of the developments which are taking place. They fill my mind out of all comparison with anything else.'

The 'developments' to which the Prime Minister referred centred not only on the growing expansion of Communism in the Third World, and particularly in Southeast Asia, but on the increasing capability of the Soviet Union to back up its political moves with the threat of nuclear force. By the beginning of 1954 the Russians had a small stockpile of atomic bombs, and their rapid rate of progress in the field of nuclear weapons indicated that they would soon be in a position to deploy hydrogen bombs as well. The capability of the Soviet Union to deliver such weapons had always lagged well behind that of the United States — in 1954 the only jet bomber in service with the Soviet Air Force was the Ilyushin II-28, a twin-jet aircraft roughly comparable with the B-45 Tornado or the Canberra — the traditional flypast of military hardware at Moscow's Tushino airport on 1 May 1954 revealed that the Russians might be catching up.

Two new Soviet jet bombers, both of them modern designs and clearly capable of carrying nuclear weapons, flew overhead with an escort of MiG fighters. The aircraft were obviously prototypes, but they bore no comparison with the 'one-off' experimental (and unsuccessful) bomber prototypes which had appeared over Tushino in previous years. The first, a large, swept-wing machine with four jet engines buried in the wing roots, was allocated the NATO code-name 'Bison'; its real designation was Myasishchev M-4, and it had already been ordered into production. So had the second prototype bomber, a twin-jet swept-wing aircraft that seemed to be the equivalent of the B-47. This was given the code-name 'Badger' and was later discovered to be a product of the Andrei N. Tupolev design bureau, which had produced the B-29 copy.

There was to be a further revelation at the 1955 Tushino display with the unveiling of another new swept-wing strategic bomber, this time powered by four big turboprop engines. Codenamed 'Bear' by NATO, its real designation was Tupolev Tu-95 and it was the true linear descendant of the Tu-4 copy of the B-29. The Russians had come a long way in less than a decade.

Stalin, who had died in March 1953, had bequeathed to his successor the basic ingredients of a strategic air force and a nuclear weapon, and the first Soviet long-range jet bombers were beginning to come off the production line as the two principal contenders for power in the USSR, Georgi Malenkov and Nikita Khrushchev engaged in a bitter struggle over the succession. Khrushchev was to emerge victorious by the end of 1954, and over the next decade was to launch the Soviet Union into a global role with forays into the Middle East, Africa, Southeast Asia and the Caribbean. To back his international moves he required a credible deterrent to offset the US strategic threat, and this was to be based on the strategic bomber until the advent of reliable intercontinental ballistic missiles in the early 1960s.

However, the Soviet Union would not possess enough of the new jet bombers to present a credible threat to the United States and NATO until the end of the 1950s, and in the meantime the USA held all the nuclear cards. The policy of the nuclear deterrent had already been clearly defined by President Eisenhower as the need 'to be constantly ready, on an instantaneous basis, to inflict greater loss upon the enemy than he could reasonably hope to inflict upon us.' This view matched the opinion of US Secretary of State John Foster Dulles, although the two did not agree on how the deterrent force should be implemented.

In the summer of 1953, during a discussion with Eisenhower on post-Korea foreign policy, Dulles had advocated that the United States increase its nuclear weapons production and withdraw its troops from Asia and Europe; the nuclear threat would be enough to ensure stability. Eisenhower had rejected this, believing that the first task was to educate the American people about the horrors of nuclear war, 'otherwise we will drift aimlessly, probably to our own eventual destruction.' At the same time, he continued in a memorandum to Dulles, 'We should patiently point out that any group of people, such as the men in the Kremlin, who are aware of the great destructiveness of these weapons — and who still decline to make any honest effort towards international control by collective action — must be fairly assumed to be contemplating their aggressive use.' Only then, Eisenhower thought, would the average citizen recognise the need for a nuclear deterrent.

Responding to Dulles' recommendation for a defence policy based on a massive overkill capacity, Eisenhower agreed that such a capacity would constitute a deterrent, but warned that 'if the contest to maintain this relative position should have to continue indefinitely, the cost would either drive us to war or into some form of dictatorial government. In such circumstances, we should be forced to consider whether or not our duty to future generations did not require us to *initiate* war at the most propitious moment that we could designate.' In short, Eisenhower was considering whether the best way to deal with the Soviet nuclear threat might be to eliminate it while it was still in its embryo stage by means of a pre-emptive atomic attack — in other words, a first strike. But it was no more than a consideration, and Eisenhower did not advocate such a step. Nevertheless, the possibility remained in his mind, and he was to voice it again in the summer of 1954,when the French were being beaten by the communist Viet Minh forces in Indo-China.

In May 1954, the French came to believe that the Viet Minh were about to receive massive aid from Red China in the shape of squadrons of jet aircraft, which the French completely lacked in that theatre, and wanted assurances that the United States would intervene with its military forces if such a thing occurred. The options for such intervention were studied in depth by the Joint Chiefs of Staff, the National Security Council, the State Department and the White House. The Joint Chiefs of Staff, who had made a set of unauthorised promises to the French, had already worked out a war plan and were ready to take action — not in Indo-China, but in China itself. The National Security Council's view, expressed by Robert Cutler, the chairman of its planning board, was that 'there was little use discussing any "defense" of Southeast Asia; that US power should be directed against the source of the peril, which was, at least in the first instance, China and that in this connection atomic weapons should be used.'

Secretary of State Dulles, who viewed any Chinese intervention in Indo-China as tantamount to a declaration of war against the United States, urged the President to get a resolution through Congress immediately, authorising him to respond to such intervention as he saw fit. Eisenhower, Robert Cutler recorded, told Dulles that if he were to go to Congress for authority he would not ask for halfway measures. If the situation warranted it, there would be declared a state of war with China, and there might be a strike on Russia. The President watered down his statement somewhat by commenting that he would never permit the United States to act unilaterally in Indo-China, but if the occasion arose to act in concert with Allies 'there should be no halfway measures or frittering around. The Navy and Air Force should go in with full power, using new weapons, and strike at air bases and ports in mainland China.'

Eisenhower, however, believed that an atomic attack on China would inevitably bring Russia into the conflict, so if there were to be a pre-emptive strike Russia and China would have to be attacked simultaneously. To the Joint Chiefs of Staff he had this to say: 'I want you to carry this question home with you. Gain such a victory, and what do you do with it? Here would be a great area from the Elbe to Vladivostok torn up and destroyed, without government, without its communications, just an area of starvation and disaster. I ask you what would the civilised world do about it? I repeat there is no victory except through our imaginations.'

His views on pre-emptive nuclear action were expressed again later, this time at a news conference. 'I don't believe there is such a thing; and, frankly, I wouldn't even listen to anyone seriously that came in and talked about such a thing . . . It seems to me that when, by definition, a term is just ridiculous in itself, there is no use in going any further.'

Thirty years on, there are those who might claim, with some

justification, that the 'arms race' falls into just that category of ridiculous military concepts for which Eisenhower had no time.

As it turned out, there was no Red Chinese intervention in Indo-China; there was no need of it, for the Viet Minh under Ho Chi Minh and the redoubtable General Giap were doing all that was necessary to drive the French into a corner from which there was no escape. But in the summer of 1954 the threat of Chinese — and possibly joint Sino-Soviet — action in south-east Asia seemed very real, and during this period the USAF was held on a high degree of alert.

In Britain, Third Air Force and SAC units trained by day and night with an increased intensity that brought strong protests from local communities adjacent to the major air bases. At Greenham Common the base commander was inundated with more than 1,000 letters from the residents of nearby Newbury, who complained that the constant B-47 operations made life seem like 'hell with the lid off'. At Upper Heyford, members of the local populace voiced fears that there might be a repetition, with more disastrous consequences, of an accident that occurred on 5 February 1954, when a B-47 crashed in Stoke Wood, a mile and a half from the end of the main runway.

The first atomic weapons were introduced to USAF bases in Britain during 1954, mainly as a result of the knowledge that the Soviet Union was starting to deploy her own weapons and would soon have the means to deliver them. The RAF, too, was building up its stockpile, although at a very slow rate, and this was something that troubled President Eisenhower. For several years he had been urging the creation of a European defence community, with an all-European army that was to include a rearmed Germany. Churchill opposed the idea, and in an attempt to persuade him to change his mind Eisenhower offered to supply atomic weapons to the British so that the RAF could effectively provide a deterrent for the EDC. What Eisenhower really meant, according to Dulles, was that he did not wish to see only American aircrews take punishment in delivering nuclear weapons to their targets, should the dreadful need ever arise.

To some degree, the emphasis had been on building up a stockpile of tactical, rather than strategic, nuclear weapons in

Britain. By mid-1954 nuclear weapons components were under secure storage at Sculthorpe, where the B-45 Tornados of the 47th Bomb Wing were based, at Woodbridge and Wethersfield, homes of the 20th Fighter-Bomber Wing's F-84Gs, and at Bentwaters, as well as at the SAC bases. The F-84G version of the Thunderjet, with an uprated engine, had given the USAF a tactical nuclear capability; atomic weapons development had advanced a considerable distance in the USA since 1950 and the device carried by the F-84G, although still bulky, weighed only 2,000 pounds — one-fifth the weight of the Hiroshima bomb.

At Bentwaters, the 81st Fighter-Bomber Wing had begun to receive F-84F Thunderstreaks in April 1954. The F-84F was essentially a swept-wing version of the Thunderjet but could carry up to three times its predecessor's weapons load, and at higher speeds. The 81st FBW was fully equipped with F-84Fs by the beginning of 1955, and the 20th FBW also began to receive Thunderstreaks later in the year.

It should be stressed that at no time was there any danger of an accidental explosion of stored weapons, for the simple reason that the component parts necessary to produce a nuclear explosion were always kept in widely separate storage igloos, as the hardened dome-shaped bunkers were called. To understand this point fully, it is necessary to include here a brief description of how nuclear weapons work — and of why they will not work under certain circumstances. The description refers to nuclear and not thermonuclear weapons; the latter had still to be deployed in 1954 and will be discussed later.

An atomic explosion is caused by the fission of heavy elements such as the U235 isotope of uranium and the P239 isotope of plutonium. To trigger a fission reaction it is necessary to assemble a large enough mass of U235 or P239 to ensure that a sufficient number of the high-energy neutron particles that are generated by the normal steady fission process taking place in the raw material do not escape from the surface of the mass, but collide with other atoms, causing these to break up in turn and release more neutrons. If the process creates more neutrons than can be consumed, a chain reaction of ever-increasing intensity is set up. Since each fission of a U235 or

P239 atom liberates huge amounts of energy, the result is a powerful explosion.

The minimum amount of fissile material required to sustain a chain reaction is known as the critical mass, and is around 25 pounds of P239 or 100 pounds of U235. The mere creation of a critical mass, however, is not enough to produce a nuclear explosion sufficient for military purposes, because the sheer magnitude of the reaction will tend to blow the assembly apart before a large amount of its material has been consumed by the energies liberated in the fission process.

In early atomic weapons, this problem was overcome by using the so-called 'gun' principle, in which a sub-critical mass of fissile material was fired at a target made of the same material. Their combined mass exceeded the critical value, while the energy imparted by the gun to the moving mass was sufficient to keep the two sections in contact while the reaction built up. In the late 1940s, however, following a further series of nuclear tests by the Americans, the more sophisticated 'implosion' system was brought into use. In this case, a spherical fissile mass — in other words, a nuclear capsule — of sub-critical size is surrounded by a layer of high-explosive 'lenses'; when the latter are fired at precisely the same instant, the fissile mass is compressed to produce a super-critical mass in which the chain reaction can begin.

Until the mid-1950s SAC aircraft were not flown with nuclear weapons in the strike configuration — that is, with the nuclear capsule married to the rest of the weapon — and as a result a number of potentially dangerous accidents were averted. On 13 February 1950, for example, a Convair B-36 en route from Eielson AFB, Alaska, to Carswell AFB in Texas developed engine trouble and descended into icing conditions at 8,000 feet after three engines were shut down. The weapon it carried, containing a dummy nuclear capsule for training purposes, was jettisoned into the Pacific off British Columbia and the high-explosive element detonated. The B-36 crashed on Vancouver Island after it had been abandoned by its crew.

On 11 April 1950 a B-29 left Kirtland AFB in New Mexico at 21.30 hours local time and crashed into a mountain three minutes later, killing its crew. Its bomb case was demolished and the HE element burned in the ensuing fire, but the nuclear capsule was not fitted and there was no contamination.

This was followed, on 13 July 1950, by an incident in which a B-50, flying on a training sortie at 7,000 feet on a clear day from Biggs AFB in Texas, suddenly nose-dived into the ground near Lebanon, Ohio, killing its 16-man crew. Its weapon's HE element detonated, but no nuclear capsule was aboard. Then, on 5 August 1950, a B-29 carrying a weapon but no capsule had two runaway propellers and was unable to retract is undercarriage on takeoff from Fairchild-Suisun AFB, California: the B-29 crashed and burned. Nineteen aircrew and rescue personnel were killed (including General Travis, after whom the base was renamed) and the weapon's HE element detonated fifteen minutes after the crash. Finally, on 10 November 1950, a B-50 on an overwater flight outside the United States jettisoned a weapon from 10,500 feet. The weapon did not have its nuclear capsule fitted and the HE was seen to detonate.

No further incidents involving USAF atomic weapons were recorded until 1956, by which time both weapons and aircraft were a good deal more advanced. Nevertheless, the USAF still went to great pains to keep the capsules and the HE elements separate, as was shown in an incident on 10 March 1956 when one of four B-47s on a non-stop flight from McDill AFB in Florida to a base in Turkey failed to make its second tanker rendezvous over the Mediterranean. The aircraft carried two nuclear capsules in sealed carrier cases, but no HE element. The B-47 went down into the sea when its fuel ran out, and despite an intensive search no trace of the aircraft, crew or capsules was ever found.

The next incident involved a B-47 at one of 7th Air Division's British bases. On 27 July 1956, an unarmed Stratojet was practising roller landings at Lakenheath when it went out of control and slid off the runway into the bomb dump. Its fuel tanks exploded, killing the crew, and the ensuing fire enveloped a storage igloo containing several nuclear weapons in storage configuration, with no nuclear capsules present. The HE elements in themselves might have caused a sizeable explosion, but the heat- and blast-resistant nature of the igloo prevented damage to the interior and the HE did not detonate.

These incidents serve to illustrate that, even in the early days of

the nuclear deterrent, public fears concerning the accidental deto-
nation of nuclear weapons were unfounded. Atomic weapons in
storage could not possibly be detonated accidentally; an ordinary
high-explosive bomb dump was potentially far more lethal.

Thermonuclear weapons presented a different problem
requiring a different set of safety precautions. The only method
of initiating a thermonuclear (fusion) reaction is by using a
fission trigger, because only a nuclear explosion can produce
the required combination of temperature and pressure. The
deuterium and tritium isotopes of hydrogen (hence the popular
term 'H-bomb') then combine to produce the minimum tem-
peratures — about 80 million degrees centigrade — needed to
kindle the thermonuclear reaction. However, tritium is a
cryogenic material which has to be stored within a few degrees
of absolute zero, and this gave both American and Soviet
scientists some headaches when it came to devising a thermonuclear weapon that could be air-delivered.

In the end, both came up with the same solution. By surrounding a fission trigger with a blanket of lithium-6, they
created what was essentially a tritium factory at the heart of a
nuclear explosion. Lithium-6 was converted into tritium when
bombarded by the neutrons released by the nuclear trigger,
and had the advantage of being relatively easy to handle and
store. But the problems were by no means over; although the
basic device was relatively small — the amount of lithium-6
required to create a thermonuclear weapon being in the region
of 200 pounds — the safety precautions that were necessary to
produce an operational weapon that could safely be handled by
non-scientific personnel were so exhaustive that they resulted
in a much larger and bulkier assembly than had been envisaged
at first.

The designers of such a weapon had to assume that critical
components in the fusing, arming and triggering chain of a
thermonuclear weapon might one day fail, and they had to devise
systems which would continue to operate safely and satisfactorily
even if two related or independent faults occurred at the same
time. The result of this fail-safe policy was that each thermonuclear weapon was fitted with a complex series of safety locks,
all of which had to be tripped before the weapon could detonate.

These factors contributed to making the development of a deliverable thermonuclear weapon a protracted affair, and at one point it appeared that the Russians were in the lead. In November 1955 they tested a device with a yield of about two megatons, and US Intelligence sources confirmed that it had been air-dropped — a capability the Americans did not then possess. When the Russians undertook a series of similar tests in March 1956 the Americans accelerated their own nuclear test programme with the aim of devising a configuration that would fit into an aircraft and, in the longer term, a warhead that could be used in a long-range missile.

Operation Redwing, a series of tests involving more than a dozen nuclear explosions at proving grounds in the Pacific, began on 5 May 1956, and on 21 May a ten-megaton bomb was successfully released over Bikini Atoll by a Boeing B-52 Strato-fortress, the latest and largest jet bomber to join Strategic Air Command. By the late 1950s the combination of the B-52 and the thermonuclear bomb was to give SAC an unparalleled and devastating strike potential.

In other areas, however, there were indications that the Russians might still be in the lead. They had nothing to compare with the B-52 in the manned strategic bomber field, but in the spring of 1956 Nikita Khrushchev boasted that the Soviet Union would soon have guided missiles with H-bomb warheads capable of hitting any point in the world. The Americans took the boast seriously; it was known that the Russians had tested a rocket known as the R-7, developed from the wartime German V-2, and US Intelligence quite wrongly asserted that R-7s were rolling off the production lines like cars in Detroit. In fact the R-7 — which was to be used as the basis for the booster rocket that would launch the world's first earth satellite, Sputnik I, eighteen months later — would have been completely ineffective as a long-range military missile, but the vision of giant Soviet rockets delivering enough H-bombs to burn America from coast to coast was enough to send a shudder of panic through even the most hard-headed members of the Joint Chiefs of Staff.

The massive Douglas C-124 Globemaster II was the USAF's standard heavy-lift transport aircraft during most of the 1950s, and made possible the rapid supply of spares and other equipment – including Thor IRBMs – to British bases from the USA.

The Lockheed F-80 Shooting Star was the USAF's first operational jet fighter, and was deployed to USAFE bases via the United Kingdom in the summer of 1948. It could carry a substantial weapons load in the fighter-bomber role, as this photograph shows.

The Lockheed T-33 jet trainer was a two-seat development of the F-80. In the 1950s most US air bases in Britain had at least one of these aircraft for aircrew refresher work and also fast communications.

In 1950, Republic F-84 Thunderjets of the 20th Fighter-Bomber Wing were deployed to Manston in Kent to provide fighter escort for SAC bombers. The F-84G was the first aircraft in the world capable of carrying a tactical atomic bomb. The dramatic shot above shows an F-84G harmonizing its .5-inch machine guns at night. The F-84F Thunderstreak (below) was a swept-wing version of the F-84G, which it replaced. The 81st Fighter-Bomber Wing was the first to equip with it in the UK, followed by the 20th. Photo shows an F-84F firing a salvo of five-inch high-velocity aircraft rockets.

At the end of 1954 the 406th Fighter Interceptor Group at Manston began re-equipping with all-weather F-86D Sabres; these aircraft were fitted with an advanced fire-control system and 24 'Mighty Mouse' anti-aircraft rockets, seen being fired here.

The North American T-39 Sabreliner was widely used as a VIP transport throughout the USAF in the 1960s, and was a frequent commuter between USAF bases in the UK and Europe.

Suddenly, the need to know exactly what the Russians were up to assumed critical importance. Air reconnaissance was the answer, and the United Kingdom was the ideal location for the aircraft that were to carry out this task.

4

The High Cold War

THE GATHERING OF electronic intelligence dates back to the earliest days of radar, and was a key factor in the air operations of both sides during World War II. In 1942, for example, knowledge of the frequencies on which German search and tracking radars operated enabled the British to develop effective countermeasures against them. Not only was such knowledge vital to the effectiveness of the Allied strategic bombing offensive, but it also contributed in no small measure to the success of the Allied landings in Normandy. On 5 June 1944 two squadrons of RAF Lancasters flew fixed patterns over the English Channel for several hours, dropping bundles of 'window' — strips of tinfoil cut exactly to the wavelength of the German warning radar — and succeeded in making the enemy believe that the D-Day invasion was taking place miles from the actual landing zones. With the advent of more advanced radar systems after 1945 the gathering of electronic intelligence (elint) assumed even greater importance, and the probing of the other side's radar defences by both the Russians and the Western Allies subsequently became a vital aspect of the cold war. It was not without its cost; between 1945 and 1960, the Americans lost at least fifteen aircraft and sixty-nine aircrew on operations of this type.

Here are some of the recorded incidents:

1950
8 April   PB4Y Privateer of US Navy Patrol Squadron VP-26, with ten men on board, was shot down by Soviet fighters over the Baltic. There were no survivors.

1953

18 January   Lockheed P2V Neptune of Navy Squadron VP-22, on an elint mission over the Formosa Strait, was shot down off Swatow Island by Chinese anti-aircraft fire. Rescue operations were hampered by shore battery gunfire and high seas, the latter causing a Coast Guard rescue aircraft to crash on take-off. Total losses from the incident were eleven men, seven of them from the P2V crew.

29 July   USAF RB-50 operating out of Yokota Air Base in Japan was attacked by Soviet MiG-15s at 0615 hours while cruising at 21,000 feet over the Sea of Japan, forty miles from the Russian coast in international airspace. The RB-50's gunners returned the fire, but one wing of the aircraft broke away and it spun towards the sea, breaking up as it fell. One crew member escaped by parachute and was picked up by an American destroyer after drifting for several hours in his life-raft; the other fourteen perished.

1954

9 September   P2V Neptune of the US Navy's Patrol Squadron 19, on an intelligence-gathering mission over international waters, was attacked by two MiG-15s and forced to ditch off the Siberian coast. Nine of the crew escaped and were subsequently rescued, but one was lost with the aircraft.

1955

22 June   P2V Neptune, this time belonging to US Navy Squadron VP-9, was attacked by two MiG-15s while patrolling in the vicinity of the Aleutians; the fighters set fire to the Neptune's starboard engine and forced the aircraft to crash-land on St Lawrence Island. This time there were no casualties.

1956

22 August   Long-range Martin P4M Mercator, on night patrol out of Iwakuni, Japan, with thirteen men on board, reported that it was under attack by aircraft over international waters thirty-two miles off the coast of China and was not heard from again. Aircraft and surface ships, carrying out an intensive search, found wreckage, empty life rafts and the bodies of two crew members. The Mercator belonged to Electronic Counter-measures Squadron VQ-1, which had been formed a year earlier.

The high proportion of US Navy aircraft involved in these incidents is explained by the fact that the USN's elint missions were usually flown over the sea, whereas USAF missions were flown over the territory of NATO or other Allied countries around the periphery of the Soviet Union. Aircraft over the sea were vulnerable to interception and attack, and there were seldom survivors or witnesses. Interceptions over land produced all manner of complications, as demonstrated by a classic incident involving a USAF C-130 Hercules on 2 September 1958.

The Hercules, attached to the 7406th Support Squadron and normally based at Rhein-Main, near Frankfurt, carried advanced elint equipment and a crew of seventeen, thirteen of whom were signals specialists. That morning it had taken off from Adana, in southern Turkey, to fly a mission that involved intercepting and identifying signals from the network of Soviet radar stations to the north of the Black Sea and in Armenia and Georgia. Under circumstances which are still unclear it entered Soviet airspace and was shot down. The radio chatter of the Russian fighter pilots was recorded by a NATO monitoring station in Turkey and produced evidence when the Russians denied all knowledge of the American aircraft. After a lot of diplomatic wrangling the Russians eventually admitted that the Hercules had crashed in their territory and returned the bodies of six of the missing crew members.

Great Britain's geographical position made it an ideal base for surveillance flights along the northern fringes of the Soviet Union, from Murmansk across the Barents Sea as far as Severnaya Zemlya, and new impetus was given to these activities in 1949, when Russia exploded her first nuclear device. At that time Russia's strategic bomber arm, the Dalnaya Aviatsiya, was equipped with the obsolescent Tupolev Tu-4, but it was known that more modern derivatives were being tested which, armed with first-generation Soviet atomic bombs, would have the range to threaten the continental United States.

First and foremost, therefore, the Americans needed to keep surveillance on existing Soviet bomber bases on the edge of the Arctic, and to pinpoint any new ones that were being built. They also needed to identify the types of radar that were coming into service in a new chain that was being erected across the whole of the Soviet Arctic region; this was not difficult to do, for radio equipment developed in Britain and the USA during the war was already capable of distinguishing between the pulses emitted by long-range search radars and those associated with shorter-range fighter control radars. It was soon discovered that there were close parallels between the Russian system and the German air defence system of 1944–45 — hardly surprising, given that the Soviet network was being set up with the aid of German technicians and that much of the equipment it used was developed from German designs.

Like its German counterpart of 1944–45, the Soviet system relied on an overlapping chain of early warning stations, each subdivided into fighter control sectors; like the Germans, the Russians only used a limited number of VHF channels to control their fighters. The four Soviet channels in use up to 1960 were well monitored and all of them could be jammed by a single piece of countermeasures equipment, known in British service as Green Palm, which emitted a high-pitched wail.

Early electronic surveillance flights by USAF aircraft from bases in the United Kingdom were carried out by RB-29 and RB-50 Superfortresses. The shortcomings of the RB-29 as a reconnaissance aircraft operating in a hostile environment were revealed in tragic fashion in the early months of the Korean War, when the type suffered appalling losses at the hands of the MiG-15: neither it nor the RB-50 were fast enough to escape, even when hostile fighters were detected at long range, and surveillance operations with these aircraft from the UK were flown well clear of Soviet airspace.

During 1947–50 there were numerous short incursions into Soviet-controlled airspace, but these mainly involved flights into eastern Europe by the RAF, using de Havilland Mosquito PR.34s of Nos. 540, 541 and 543 Squadrons operating out of RAF Benson and Wyton in the United Kingdom and various forward bases in Germany. The Mosquito's ceiling of 43,000 feet and maximum speed of over 400 mph made it immune to interception by the piston-engined Soviet fighter types then in service, but when the MiG-15 began to reach the Russian interceptor squadrons in eastern Europe missions of this type ceased.

From 1951 overflights of Soviet territory from British bases were carried out by Convair RB-36Ds. Seventeen of these massive aircraft were built and seven more converted from the standard B-36B strategic bomber version. Their huge weapons bays converted into pressurised compartments housing fourteen cameras, surveillance equipment and six specialist crew members (the RB-36D carried 22 crew instead of the B-36D's 16). No details of the overflights made by these aircraft have been released, but with a ceiling of more than 42,000 feet in lightened condition, a top speed of 435 mph over the target and a range of 8,000 miles, they were quite capable of photographing airfields and installations as far afield as Severnaya Zemlya.

These long-range excursions resulted, in November 1951, in the Soviet Aviation Ministry issuing an urgent specification for an all-weather fighter fitted with a long-range search radar, the Izumrud (Emerald) airborne interception radar carried by existing Soviet fighter types being quite inadequate for interception of the American reconnaissance aircraft. It was not until 1956 that such an aircraft — the Yakovlev Yak-25 'Flashlight' — entered service with the Soviet Air Force's interceptor squadrons, and until that time the reconnaissance flights continued with impunity, the RB-36Ds eventually being replaced by later-model RB-36Hs.

In 1952 the USAF's reconnaissance capability received a boost with the arrival in Britain of the first RB-45 high-altitude reconnaissance variants of the B-45 Tornado tactical light bomber. A year earlier RB-45s had been evaluated under operational conditions when two aircraft were shipped out to Korea with Reconnaissance Detachment A of the 84th Bombardment Squadron. Attached to the 91st Squadron, these aircraft managed to outrun and outmanoeuvre the MiGs in north-western Korea for several months, but on 9 April 1951 four enemy fighters got on the tail of an RB-45 and pursued it until they had discharged all their ammunition — amazingly without securing any hits. From then on, daylight operations by the RB-45s were flown with fighter escort, but after a particularly harrowing experience on 9 November 1951, when an unescorted RB-45 was intercepted by nine MiG-15s and only escaped because of abysmally poor gunnery, the RB-45s were restricted to night operations.

The RB-45 arrived in England, then, with the knowledge that its usefulness would be handicapped by its performance; the majority of reconnaissance sorties were flown at night, and those over central Europe. Some RB-45s carried Royal Air Force markings for a time, presumably to disguise their arrival in England and to delude the potential enemy into thinking that they were Canberras, to which they bore a superficial resemblance, though it is unlikely that the Russians were fooled.

By 1954 much of the USAF's long-range reconnaissance task from the United Kingdom had passed to the RB-47E Stratojet, which was equipped with seven cameras for day and night photography; also flown from Britain were the RB-47H and RB-47K, which were modified for electronic intelligence gathering and had a pressurised compartment containing three electronics specialists in the bomb-bay.

In 1954–55 some RB-47Es made penetrations of up to 300 miles behind the Iron Curtain to gather photographic intelligence, mostly at night, but the B-47 suffered from a relatively low ceiling of 40,000 feet and operations of this type ceased with the advent of modern Russian night fighters.

Ceiling was the main problem. Speed was secondary to the need to outclimb any hostile interceptor. The RAF had solved the problem to some degree early in the 1950s, when stripped down de Havilland Venoms based in Germany were used to make penetration flights at altitudes of up to 55,000 feet. However, the Venom suffered from a lack of range, and its use was essentially an interim measure until the arrival of the Canberra PR.3. This photo-reconnaissance version of the RAF's first jet bomber entered service with No. 541 Squadron at Benson in 1953 and was succeeded by two further versions, the PR.7 and PR.9. The latter could fly at 55,000 feet with a useful operation load and was to remain in RAF service until 1982.

In the mid-1950s the Russians were extremely touchy about American intelligence-gathering operations, and the reason was not hard to find. In the spring of 1956, a USAF unit known as the 1st Weather Observation Squadron (Provisional) at Watertown, Nevada, had received the first examples of a radical new aircraft that was to alter the whole concept of air reconnaissance: the Lockheed U-2. Virtually a powered glider, with a wingspan of eighty feet and fitted with a modified version of the well-tried J-57 jet engine, the U-2 was the answer to the urgent USAF requirement for an aircraft capable of penetrating deep into Soviet territory at an altitude that would make it immune to interception by the fighters then in service.

The initial production batch of ten U-2s were in fact used for high-altitude weather reconnaissance and sampling of radiation levels in the upper atmosphere, but subsequent aircraft were assigned to SAC's 4028th and 4080th Strategic Reconnaissance Squadrons. These squadrons were based on Laughlin Air Force Base, Texas, and Ramey AFB in Puerto Rico, but detachments were sent to Lakenheath in Britain, Wiesbaden in Germany and Incirlik in Turkey, and during the autumn of 1956 a series of probing flights were carried out over the fringes of Soviet territory from these bases. On 17 November 1956 one U-2 exploded in mid-air near Kaiserlautern while operating from Wiesbaden, killing Lockheed pilot Howard Carey; there had been two previous accidents that year, both in the United States.

When the preliminary probing flights ended without incident, the U-2s began to undertake deep penetration flights into the heart of the Soviet Union, photographing air bases, missile sites under construction, factories, industrial complexes, radar sites and other objectives of interest to SAC's target planners.

Meanwhile, the presence of U-2s at Lakenheath had not gone unnoticed, as the USAF had doubtless hoped that it might, the Americans having reckoned without one of the more widespread hobbies of the young British male — aircraft spotting. After April 1956, when the mysterious unmarked aircraft first put in an appearance, Britain's aviation periodicals were deluged with letters from spotters who were avid to know the

aircraft's identity and mission. For a long time the USAF
refused to comment, but it finally issued a statement to the
effect that the machine was a Lockheed U-2 and that it was
engaged in gathering information 'relating to clear air
turbulence, convective clouds, wind shear and the jet stream
. . . cosmic rays and the concentration of certain elements in
the atmosphere, including ozone and water vapour.'

The spotters were not fooled. As the months passed there
was a growing realisation that the mysterious U-2's activities
might not be concerned solely with research, and that in some
respects this strange machine, with its midnight blue anti-
corrosion paint finish and total lack of identification markings,
might be the proverbial wolf in sheep's clothing. Why else
would a simple weather reconnaissance aircraft be so closely
guarded from unauthorised eyes? In June 1957 the journal
Flying Review ventured the opinion that 'it is possible that U-2s
are flying across the Iron Curtain taking aerial photographs or
probing radar defences'.

Flying Review had hit the nail squarely on the head.
Throughout 1957 the U-2s cruised singly over the Soviet Union
at altitudes of 65,000 feet or more, apparently undetected by
the Soviet defences. Because of the extreme heights at which
they flew, their turbojets were fed by a specially developed fuel
whose boiling point was 150 degrees centigrade at sea level.
Early U-2As had a range of about 2,000 miles, but the U-2Bs
that followed could fly 4,000 miles with the help of underwing
fuel tanks, and under operational conditions range could be
extended still further by deliberately flaming-out the J-75 turbojet and gliding for long distances, the engine being restarted
only when the aircraft reached a dangerously low level. On one
occasion a U-2 on an air test over the Caribbean Sea from its
base on Puerto Rico suffered an engine failure and made a
successful emergency landing on Bermuda after gliding 300
miles.

By 1958 the Russians were clearly aware of the U-2 flights,
for fighters were sent up to intercept the elusive intruders. U-2
pilots began to report attempted interceptions by MiG-19s and
the latest MiG-21s, but the Soviet fighters were unable to reach
the heights at which the U-2s operated. They would zoom-

climb to 60,000 feet, fire their cannon at the top of the trajectory, then stall in the rarified air and fall away. Yet because of
the severe loss of prestige that would have resulted from an
open admission that American aircraft were roving over the
Soviet Union at will, the Russians never made any form of
protest; the first indication that they knew exactly what was
happening came by way of some obscure references in the Red
Air Force journal *Sovietskaya Aviatsiya*, which admitted that
Russian air defence officers were seriously worried about the
threat to Soviet security posed by American reconnaissance
aircraft. The journal made a direct reference to the U-2 in
September 1958, when it stated: 'The U-2 lacks all identification markings indicating its mission . . . the U-2 has been
accepted by US Strategic Air Command and has made
repeated flights from Wiesbaden, West Germany.' There was
no mention of U-2s operating from British bases.

In 1959 and the early months of 1960, although the number
of operational sorties was somewhat reduced, the U-2s turned
their attention to the IRBM and ICBM sites which were
springing up all over the Soviet Union. In April 1960 the US
Central Intelligence Agency received information that the Russians had completed a very advanced missile site near
Sverdlovsk, and a U-2 of the special CIA 10–10 Squadron was
detailed to photograph it, together with the rocket research
centre at Tyuratam and the air and naval bases at Archangelsk
and Murmansk.

The U-2 selected for the mission was flown from Incirlik to
Peshawar, in Pakistan, at the end of April 1960; its serial
number was 56–6689, and it had operated out of Lakenheath
on a number of previous occasions. It was not a favourite
aircraft among the small band of CIA U-2 pilots, who had
encountered fuel transfer problems while changing from one
tank to another in the air as well as several other annoying
snags in flying this particular machine. Nevertheless, it was the
only example that could be spared for this mission, so at 0620
local time on the morning of 1 May 1960 it took off from
Peshawar and climbed out over northern Afghanistan on the
first stage of a nine-hour, 2,800-mile flight over the Soviet
Union that would terminate at nightfall on the NATO air base

of Bodø, in northern Norway. The U-2's pilot was a civilian CIA employee, Francis Gary Powers.

The rest is history. Powers' U-2 was shot down by a Soviet missile battery near Sverdlovsk; his subsequent interrogation and trial made world-wide headlines; and the U-2 incident effectively wrecked a major East-West summit conference scheduled to be held in Paris a fortnight later. Powers himself was sentenced to ten years' imprisonment in the Soviet Union, but he served only two years before being released in exchange for the Russian master spy Colonel Rudolf Abel. He was killed in a flying accident some years later.

After the Powers incident U-2 flights over the Soviet Union were suspended, but electronic reconnaissance flights around the periphery continued and it was not long before they claimed more lives. On 1 July 1960, while the Powers trial was still in progress, an RB-47H Stratojet of the 98th Strategic Reconnaissance Wing took off from Brize Norton to carry out an electronic reconnaissance of the Barents Sea, and in particular, of the highly sensitive Soviet nuclear test site on Novaya Zemlya. The aircraft carried a crew of six.

High over the Barents Sea, north of Archangelsk, the RB-47H was intercepted by a MiG-19 fighter of the Soviet 206th Air Division and — according to the Russian version — signalled to land in Soviet territory. The crew ignored the signals and the Stratojet was shot down. After ten days the Russians announced that they had picked up two survivors, First Lieutenants Freeman B. Olmstead and John R. McKane; a third crew member, Captain William A. Palm, was found dead in his dinghy. The survivors were prosecuted by the Russians, imprisoned and later repatriated.

The news brought a vigorous protest from President Eisenhower, who said: 'It should be clear to the Soviet Government that a repetition of acts of this nature cannot fail to have the most serious consequences, responsibility for which would rest on the Soviet Government alone'. The statement declared that the United States 'solemnly and vigorously protests against the unwarranted shooting down of an American airplane over international waters and the cynical failure of the Soviet Government to make its action known for a period of days during which a search for the missing men was known to be in course, in which the Soviet Government was voluntarily participating in what was apparently good faith'.

Cynical or not, the Russians knew full well that Eisenhower did not have a leg to stand on. With the U-2 affair still reverberating round the world, they held all the political propaganda cards. The world was now asking only one question: why, a mere two months after Powers went down, had the Americans been stupid enough to provoke another incident?

Unlike Powers' U-2 the RB-47 had taken off from a base in Britain, and in Parliament there was a predictable backlash from Her Majesty's Opposition. 'Never before,' wrote *Daily Mirror* parliamentary correspondent William Greig, 'have I seen Mr Macmillan [the Prime Minister] so flustered and uneasy as he was when he faced a torrent of questions from Labour and Conservative MPs on the U-2 flight and the shooting down of the RB-47. He had ranged alongside him the three Ministers vitally concerned — the Foreign Secretary, the Minister of Defence and the Air Minister. Time after time he hesitated before answering questions and turned to them for guidance and advice.

'While under fire from the Labour benches he sat huddled up with head bowed, a strange contrast to the soldierly figure he generally presents. It was clear he did not know the answers to many of the questions.'

There were two principal questions. First, had Britain been consulted about the clandestine flight from her base? The answer was plainly no, and the Prime Minister promised to consult urgently with President Eisenhower about the terms on which the bases were to be used in future. The second point was this: if the RB-47 had, in fact, been making a reconnaissance of Russian defences (as was generally assumed) even from outside territorial limits, was this legitimate? The public was divided (those who disagreed presumably never having heard of the fleet of Soviet intelligence-gathering ships on permanent station around Britain's coasts) but many of those who thought it legitimate doubted if it were prudent.

In the end, British and United States officials thrashed out an agreement in Washington whereby the British government was to have full knowledge of the programme and the purpose of American reconnaissance flights from British bases. Previous flight schedules had been examined by the RAF, but only to fit them into the overall air traffic pattern; in future they were to be examined not only from this technical aspect but also, for their political implications, by the Foreign Office. Programmes were to be submitted earlier and in more detailed form to allow time to question any specific mission; however, the question of a British veto was never discussed.

The matter was still being raised in parliament in October 1960, when, in response to one question, Harold Macmillan stated: 'As I told the House last summer, discussions were undertaken at the official level to review arrangements relating to the use by the United States forces of bases in this country. I took the opportunity of my visit to the United States to review these arrangements personally with President Eisenhower. I am satisfied that the position agreed is satisfactory from our point of view.'

Denis Healey, soon to become Defence Minister in a Labour Government, was not prepared to let the Prime Minister off the hook. Neither was Jo Grimond, leader of the Liberal Party, as the following exchange shows:

Mr Healey: 'When the House discussed these matters in the summer great concern was shown on both sides at the fact that it had been proved that it was possible for military persons — and foreign military persons at that — to take actions of great political importance from bases in this country without reference to those who carry political responsibility in Britain. Can the Prime Minister at least give the House some general principles governing the agreement and assure the House that this is no longer possible? In particular, can he assure the House, in terms, that he is now in a position to take direct responsibility for all flights of foreign military aircraft from bases in this country?'

Mr Macmillan: 'No. I am satisfied that under the arrangements, as we have been through them, everything that takes place will be fully known to the responsible political heads of both countries.'

Mr Grimond: 'Can the Prime Minister tell us whether the Government are informed of all reconnaissance flights from this country before they take place, and whether they have any right of veto over such flights?'

Mr Macmillan: 'It would be quite wrong to publish the details of the arrangements we have made, but I can say that we are fully informed on both sides of everything that is proposed to be done.'

With hindsight, it seems that the fact that Prime Minister Harold Macmillan had not been briefed about the USAF reconnaissance flights was an omission on the part of the Air Ministry. There was certainly collusion between the RAF and USAF on such matters, for the RAF got up to exactly the same activity; Nos. 51 and 98 Squadrons of RAF Signals Command operated black-painted Canberras out of Watton, in Norfolk, on so-called 'ferret' missions at this time. From 1960 No. 51 also used Comet R.2 aircraft, adaptations of the famous civil jet airliner; these could carry much more sophisticated surveillance equipment than the Canberra. The squadron was still active in 1985, operating Nimrod R.1s.

The other squadron engaged in the strategic reconnaissance task was No. 543, which flew Valiant B(PR).1s from Wyton, near Huntingdon, and later Handley Page Victor B.2(SR) aircraft. In 1960 these aircraft were engaged in extensive photo-mapping of large areas of the earth's surface, an updating exercise that was essential to the operation of the inertial navigation system of the Blue Steel stand-off missile, then being developed for the RAF's deterrent force; the Americans were doing the same thing for the benefit of their own stand-off weapons such as the Hound Dog missile, and since the British and American airborne nuclear deterrents were closely inter-linked there was a frequent exchange of information.

Reconnaissance flights continued, albeit more circumspectly, while firms under government contract in the United States worked flat out to perfect a satellite reconnaissance system that would eventually become operational in 1963. Meanwhile, in August 1962 American reconnaissance activities in the United Kingdom once more hit the headlines with the sudden arrival at Upper Heyford of three U-2s; the aircraft had flown from Plattsburgh, near New York, in seven hours, covering a distance of some 3,000 miles. The Americans were adamant that the U-2 detachment, which was under the command of Lieutenant-Colonel Arthur Leatherwood, USAF, had no sinister purpose; its task, they said, was to carry out a high-altitude sampling programme, a joint venture of the United States Defence Atomic Support Agency and Strategic Air Command, to determine the distribution, movement, retention and total amount of debris placed in the upper atmosphere by nuclear explosions.

The explanation was true: the Russians had recently concluded a series of nuclear tests at their Novaya Zemlya site, including one in which they had detonated a monster 57-megaton hydrogen bomb, and the U-2s' sampling activities were essential to US Intelligence in compiling an accurate estimate of the nature, yield and so on of the devices that had been exploded. The U-2s did their job and departed without any fuss.

The basic U-2A and U-2B continued to be the mainstay of Strategic Air Command's long-range reconnaissance force, and visitors to USAF bases in England have included the U-2EPX electronic surveillance version and the WU-2 weather reconnaissance aircraft. In the early 1960s, however, rumours began to circulate that the Americans were developing a potent successor to the U-2, an advanced aircraft that could penetrate Soviet airspace at extreme altitudes and speeds in excess of Mach 3 (three times the speed of sound). Such an aircraft, the Lockheed A-12, flew in April 1962, but its existence was not revealed officially for two years, and even then it was claimed to be a long-range interceptor.

In reality, although an interceptor version was proposed, the aircraft's role was strategic photographic and electronic reconnaissance, and as the SR-71A — unofficially dubbed Blackbird — it entered service with the 9th Strategic Reconnaissance Wing at Beale Air Force Base, California, in January 1966. Thereafter, detachments of single SR-71As operated worldwide from bases including Mildenhall, in Suffolk.

The SR-71A is capable of flying at 100,000 feet and can hold a speed of more than Mach 3 at 78,000 feet for one and a half hours, during which time it can cover a distance of nearly 3,000 miles. It carries a crew of two, the pilot and reconnaissance systems officer, the latter being responsible for operating a mass of highly classified equipment ranging from simple battle-field surveillance systems to high-performance multi-sensor strategic reconnaissance systems that can survey 60,000 square miles of the earth's surface in one hour from an altitude of 80,000 feet. A unique aircraft, the SR-71A incorporates design technology that is not known to have been equalled or sur-passed since. The news that the SR-71A was operating from British bases broke in August 1970, when one of these aircraft — accompanied by a pair of U-2s — refuelled at Upper Heyford on its way to carry out a surveillance mission in the Middle East.

The U-2's true successor, however — at least from the point of view of its configuration — is the Lockheed TR-1. Resem-bling the U-2, but bigger, the TR-1 is a tactical reconnaissance and battlefield surveillance aircraft. Flying at 90,000 feet over Europe, the TR-1 uses advanced radar to look many miles into hostile territory by day or night and to direct friendly strike aircraft on to potential targets. In England, the TR-1 is oper-ated by the 17th Reconnaissance Wing at Alconbury, which received its first aircraft in October 1982. The TR-1s are flown by pilots of the 95th Reconnaissance Squadron and remain under the control of Strategic Air Command.

5

Updating the Force, 1955–60

BY THE END of 1955 the USAF in Britain was concentrating
overwhelmingly on tactical operations, following a change in
Strategic Air Command's policy: the ninety-day spells of overseas temporary duty were abandoned and replaced by a continuous airborne alert in which relays of B-47s, operating from
bases in the United States and refuelling in flight, flew fixed
patterns over the Arctic. SAC's overseas bases, including those
in the United Kingdom, would now be used as post-strike
facilities.

The policy switch — a result of both economic consider-
ations and a desire to reduce overcrowding on overseas bases
that were rapidly becoming vulnerable to attack by the latest
Soviet Air Force weapons — enabled the UK-based Seventh
Air Division to reduce its strength by almost half in the early
part of 1956. Later in the year the US Army anti-aircraft and
smoke-generating units that had been deployed to Britain for
the protection of the bomber bases were withdrawn as part of
the planned reduction in the US combat force.

Detachments of B-47s continued to use the UK bases on
three-week deployments known as Reflex Alerts. Deployments
of entire SAC wings, with their full complement of 45 aircraft,
became relatively rare, and the noise pollution that had
plagued places like Newbury gradually decreased. There was
speculation that the relief was only temporary, because the
runways at both Brize Norton and Greenham Common underwent some modification and strengthening during this period,
and on 16 January 1957 the first Boeing B-52 Stratofortress to
land in Britain touched down at Brize Norton. The aircraft —

belonging to the 93rd Bomb Wing — stayed for a few days before returning to its home airfield, Castle AFB in California, and fears that it might herald the influx of a fleet of similar aircraft to UK bases were unfounded: Stratofortresses were never based in Britain except on temporary deployment to take part in exercises and bombing competitions.

Defence policy in the European context had changed radically between 1954 and 1956. In 1954 the thinking was that any all-out war would begin with a massive nuclear attack, followed by a period of 'broken-backed' warfare that would continue in desultory fashion while both sides marshalled their strategic forces for round two. By 1956, however, the nuclear deterrent was a credible force, and the launching of all-out nuclear war was becoming unthinkable: defensive policy now rested on a European 'shield' of strong conventional forces backed up by massive tactical air support. One of the primary aims of the US Redwing series of atomic tests was not to devise bigger weapons, but to produce the prototypes of weapons that could be used for tactical purposes. The Redwing tests were designed, in Eisenhower's words, 'not [to] cause more destruction — but to find out ways and means in which you can limit it, make it useful in defensive purposes . . . reduce fallout, make it more of a military weapon and less one just of mass destruction. We know we can make them big [but] we are not interested in that anymore.'

Consequently the mid-1950s saw the progressive buildup and modernisation of the Third Air Force's tactical fighter-bomber force in Britain, with the F-84F Thunderstreaks forming the primary tactical delivery system, backed up by the B-45 Tornados of the 47th Bomb Wing at Sculthorpe. In September 1955 one of the 47th's squadrons, the 86th, was detached to Alconbury near Huntingdon; work on extending and modernising this base had been in progress since 1954 and it had been activated under Third Air Force control with the arrival of the 7560th Air Base Group in March 1955.

The period 1956–58 also saw the return to British Air Ministry control of a number of bases which had been used by the USAF for several years. RAF Burtonwood, which in 1957 employed 10,000 people, was relinquished as a result of a new streamlined supply system enabling support to be given direct from depots in the USA; the Military Air Transport Service terminal remained until 1958, when it was moved to Mildenhall. Burtonwood's satellite storage complex was also relinquished in August 1957, the RAF's No. 30 Maintenance Unit moving in shortly afterwards. Full Sutton in Yorkshire, which had been designated as a reserve site for the USAF and was occupied by the 3930th Air Base Squadron from 1955 to 1957, was returned to the RAF in February 1957, while East Kirkby in Lincolnshire, another reserve field, was relinquished by the USAF in 1958.

In all, ten UK bases reverted to Air Ministry control during this period; the majority had hosted non-operational units, but Manston and Shepherd's Grove were two important exceptions. At Manston, the 406th Fighter Interceptor Wing had begun re-equipping with F-86D Sabres at the end of 1954; the F-86D was an all-weather, radar-equipped version of the F-86 day fighter and filled a serious gap in Britain's air defences. Carrying air-to-air rockets instead of cannons, it was designed to carry out radar controlled interceptions, with a Hughes AN/APX-6 radar and E.4 fire control system automatically computing a ninety-degree collision course with the target, lowering the missile pod and firing the rockets when the target was at the correct range: the twenty-four Mighty Mouse rockets, fired in an electrically controlled ripple salvo, each had the destructive force of a 75-mm artillery shell.

By 1957, however, RAF Fighter Command had begun to re-equip its night-fighter squadrons with a new and potent all-weather interceptor, the Gloster Javelin, and with the swept-wing Hawker Hunter day fighters having replaced the Command's ageing Meteors the RAF had a modern fighter force which at last made the American contribution to the air defence of Great Britain unnecessary. In May 1958, accordingly, the 406th Fighter Wing was de-activated, and in June Manston was returned to the Air Ministry.

The other Third Air Force base, Shepherd's Grove, remained the home of the 78th Fighter-Bomber Squadron's F-84F Thunderstreaks until December 1958, when it too reverted to Air Ministry control. At the same time, work ceased on two airfields — Elvington and Stansted — which had been earmarked for use by the Seventh Air Division's jet bombers under the expansion scheme of 1954. At Elvington, $2,038,000 (£724,000) had been spent on major reconstruction work, including a new east-west 9,800-foot runway that was never used by the Americans; Elvington's only post-war use, in fact, has been as a relief landing ground for RAF jet trainers from Church Fenton and Linton-on-Ouse. At Stansted, US engineers built a new 10,000-foot runway with associated hard standings, together with a parallel taxiway, before moving out in the spring of 1957; again, the runway was never used by the Americans, but their efforts proved very worthwhile for the civil airlines which have since operated out of the airport.

In June 1957 the Third Air Force's tactical striking capability received a considerable boost when the 20th Tactical Fighter Wing at Wethersfield began to exchange its F-84Fs for North American F-100D Super Sabres. The Super Sabre's evolution went back to February 1949, when the North American design team had begun to redesign the F-86 Sabre as a fighter able to reach and sustain supersonic speeds in level flight. Originally known as the Sabre 45, the new aircraft bore little resemblance to its predecessor, having a contoured, low-drag fuselage and wings and tail surfaces swept at an angle of 45 degrees. The prototype flew in May 1953 and exceeded Mach 1 on its maiden flight; a few months later it raised the world air speed record to 755.139 mph.

The first F-100A Super Sabres were delivered to the 478th Fighter Wing at George AFB, California, in September 1954, but were grounded in November following a series of unexplained crashes. It was established that the vertical tail surfaces were too small to maintain control during certain manoeuvres and so they were redesigned with 27 per cent more area, the wingspan also being increased by two feet. With these modifications the F-100A began flying operationally again in February 1955.

The F-100B, later redesignated F-107, was an all-weather fighter that flew in prototype form only, and the next production variant was the F-100C, flown for the first time in January 1955, which could carry out both ground attack and interception missions. The F-100D was the major production version, a total of 1,274 being built for the USAF Tactical Air Command and various NATO air forces; it differed from the F-100C in having an automatic pilot, jettisonable underwing pylons and further modifications to the vertical tail surfaces. The F-100D had a maximum speed of 924 mph at 36,000 feet; its service ceiling was 51,000 feet, and a combat radius with external fuel of about 700 miles meant that from bases in the eastern United Kingdom it could hit targets in Eastern Germany and Czechoslovakia. It was capable of carrying six 1,000-pound bombs, twenty-four high velocity aircraft rockets, or a single Mk. 7, Mk. 38 or Mk. 43 tactical nuclear weapon, and two squadrons were positioned at Wethersfield and a third at Woodbridge.

The second new type to arrive, in January 1958, was the Douglas RB-66 all-weather reconnaissance aircraft, which replaced the RB-45C of the 19th Squadron at Sculthorpe; soon afterwards the 47th Bombardment Wing began to exchange its elderly B-45 Tornados for B-66s, giving it a much enhanced tactical strike capability. The twin-jet B-66, a land-based development of the US Navy's A3D Skywarrior, had a maximum speed of 620 mph at 10,000 feet, a combat radius of 800 miles on internal fuel and a bomb load of 12,000 pounds. The 47th was to continue operating B-66s until June 1962, when it was deactivated.

On 10 August 1958 there was great excitement at Bentwaters when seven McDonnell F-101 Voodoos, then the world's most powerful operational fighters, arrived over the airfield with an upward bomb-burst; breaking into the circuit for a stream landing, they taxied up to the flight line to be greeted by a welcoming committee of senior Third Air Force officers, wives and civilian base employees. They had completed a transatlantic flight of 5,199 miles in eleven hours and one minute, refuelling twice from KC-135 tankers en route.

The Voodoo pilots, all drawn from the 27th Fighter-Bomber Wing at Bergstrom AFB, Texas, and commanded by Major Walter Eichelberger, were Major Brian Lincoln, Captain Charles Cleveland, Captain Carl McKenzie, Captain Howard Maree, Captain Jim Ramsey and Major Adrian Drew, and they had just established a distance record for formation flying. (There should have been eight Voodoos, but one had been forced to turn back with technical trouble.) It was Major Drew's second record in an F-101: the previous December, he had captured the world air speed record, previously held by a British Fairey Delta 2, with a speed of 1,207.6 mph at Edwards AFB, California.

The Voodoo, developed from McDonnell's abandoned XF-88 long-range escort fighter project, and first flown in September 1954, had been taken over as a project by Tactical Air Command. Three squadrons were equipped with the first production version, the F-101A, while the RF-101A reconnaissance variant equipped the 63rd Tactical Reconnaissance Wing. The next variant, the two-seat F-101B all-weather interceptor armed with high-explosive or nuclear air-to-air missiles, eventually equipped sixteen squadrons of the US Air Defense Command, while the F-101C — the type that arrived at Bentwaters on that Sunday afternoon in 1958 — was a single-seat fighter-bomber version for Tactical Air Command. It had gone into service in May 1957 with the 523rd Tactical Fighter Squadron of the 27th Fighter-Bomber Wing.

The deployment of the seven 27th FBW Voodoos to Bentwaters, apart from testing the type's capacity for rapid overseas reinforcement, was intended to familiarise base personnel with the new aircraft prior to the re-equipment of the 81st Tactical Fighter Wing. The first of the 81st's own Voodoos arrived on 4 December 1958 and equipment thereafter was rapid, enabling forty-one F-84F Thunderstreaks to be released for transfer to the Federal German Luftwaffe. The Wing's 91st and 92nd Squadrons were based at Bentwaters, with a third — the 78th — based at nearby Woodbridge.

Meanwhile, Strategic Air Command's Seventh Air Division continued to make use of six UK bases, temporary duty operations at Lakenheath having ceased in 1956. Detachments of B-47s still visited Fairford, as did a few B-36s, but the use of that base by SAC gradually declined after the end of 1955. Brize Norton continued to receive detachments of B-47s and RB-47s, the latter belonging to the 55th and 98th Strategic Reconnaissance Wings, together with their supporting

KC-97G tankers, and Greenham Common remained busy but not so noisy as before, since the B-47s on their Reflex Alert rotations did not fly continuously.

There was a nasty incident at Greenham in February 1958, when a B-47 experienced engine trouble on takeoff and the crew had to jettison two full 1,700-gallon underwing fuel tanks. These missed the designated safe area on the base, one hitting a B-47 in its dispersal and the other crashing through a hangar roof to explode inside. The resulting fire blazed for sixteen hours, despite great efforts to bring it under control with the help of fire crews from RAF Odiham; the final toll was two dead, eight injured, two B-47s totally destroyed and the hangar wrecked. The B-47 that had caused all the trouble landed safely at Brize Norton.

The other regular Seventh Air Division base, Upper Heyford, continued to host Reflex Alert B-47s, and early in 1959 two other British airfields were temporarily added to SAC's list. Bruntingthorpe, in Leicestershire, had been reactivated for USAF use in February 1957, with a new 10,000-foot runway laid for use by B-47s; while this work was in progress the base was occupied by the 3912th Air Base Squadron and later by the 3912th Combat Support Group. In January 1959 a B-47 detachment of the 100th Bomb Wing arrived and stayed until April; then, in August, the 19th Tactical Reconnaissance Squadron came over from Sculthorpe with its RB-66s. This unit formed part of the 10th Tactical Reconnaissance Wing, the rest of which was then based at Spangdahlem in Germany; in the summer of 1959, when the 10th TRW was relocated at Alconbury, Bruntingthorpe became a satellite of that airfield. The other airfield was Chelveston, which had been under USAF control since the beginning of 1953; after substantial reconstruction work, including the building of a new runway, the airfield was ready for use by SAC B-47s, which occupied it during the first six months of 1959 and were followed by a squadron of 10th TRW RB-66s.

Strategic Air Command's continuous airborne alert function had now been taken over by the B-52 Stratofortress Wings, operating from the United States, and the Reflex Alert B-47 medium bombers deployed on UK bases maintained a flight, usually of four aircraft, on fifteen minutes' readiness. This procedure was also followed by the V-Force squadrons of RAF Bomber Command, which never maintained an airborne alert force; instead, it depended on the dispersal of its bombers in clutches of four aircraft to more than thirty designated airfields around the United Kingdom during periods of alert, and on quick-reaction scramble times of two minutes or less.

By this time the first of the RAF's trio of V-Bombers, the Vickers Valiant, had been joined in service by the more advanced Avro Vulcan and Handley Page Victor. A total of twenty-five Bomber Command squadrons — including two tasked with the electronic countermeasures role and one with strategic reconnaissance — were to be equipped with the three types by 1962, and the growing proficiency of the V-Force permitted a gradual reduction of Strategic Air Command's bomber operations in the United Kingdom.

Although the British nuclear deterrent was theoretically independent, its reliance on American nuclear weapons meant it was actually nothing of the sort; in time of war Bomber Command would have operated in close conjunction with SAC, and joint procedures were worked out to ensure that the retaliatory forces of both nations would be able to survive even a surprise nuclear attack and hit back with devastating power. The joint procedures were to remain in force even after 1962, when the RAF's Vulcans and Victors were equipped with the British-designed Blue Steel stand-off missile, which was fitted with a British warhead.

Part of an article in *US Air Force and Space Digest* summed up the position admirably: 'We have become accustomed to thinking in terms of SAC alone in the retaliatory role. We overlook the fact that, in the event of actual nuclear hostilities, the first manned strike on Soviet defences will likely be spearheaded by someone else. Preceding SAC and its B-52s, and perhaps even blasting a path for it, will be the V-bomber force of the RAF — SAC's kissing cousin — Bomber Command.'

In the late 1950s, however, there were fears that the manned bomber might not survive a surprise nuclear strike. In October 1957 the Soviet Union proved to the world that it had the technological resources to place a satellite in earth orbit, and the Russians also claimed that they had successfully tested an intercontinental ballistic missile: the United States, at that time, had done neither. Some of President Eisenhower's advisers were sceptical of the Russian ICBM claim, but they were wrong; the Russians had in fact tested a prototype ICBM, the SS-6, with complete success in 1957.

The SS-6 was, in fact, the rocket that had put Sputnik I into orbit, and the secret of its success — not discovered by the West until years later — was that its hundred-foot bulk was powered by no fewer than thirty-two rocket motors clustered round its base. This was a technique the Americans had not considered — they had concentrated on multi-stage rockets. The SS-6 was primitive, but it could hurl a heavy first-generation thermonuclear warhead more than 6,000 miles, and although only a few were deployed operationally, most of those built being used as spacecraft launchers, the SS-6 filled a gap until more effective Soviet ICBMs came along.

Khrushchev's policy of concentrating on the development of missiles rather than on manned bombers appeared to be paying dividends; a medium-range ballistic weapon, the SS-3, had been in service since 1955, and with a range of 750 miles it represented a distinct threat to Western Europe.It was followed, in 1959, by the SS-4, with a range of over 1,000 miles. Khrushchev's missile-brandishing as a psycho-political force in 1957 threw the NATO alliance into a mild state of shock; its leaders were not to know that Soviet missile development had already slowed down dramatically, mainly because of a reluctance to use economic resources so badly needed elsewhere. Khrushchev, confident that the United States would not start a world war, did not commit himself to the mass production of ICBMs of which the United States thought him capable.

America's first operational medium-range missiles were in fact pilotless aircraft. The Martin TM-61A Matador, deployed in Germany from 1955, was rocket-boosted from either a hardened shelter or a mobile ramp and then flew to its target under turbojet power. Radio-guided, it had a range of about 500 miles and could be fitted with either nuclear or conventional warheads. The Matador was supplanted in 1959 by the TM-76A Mace, which had nearly double the range and carried a much larger warhead, but the snag with both these weapons was that, being subsonic, they could be intercepted.

The same pilotless bomber concept was used in the development of America's first intercontinental missile, the SM-62A Snark, which went into service in April 1957 with the 556th Strategic Missile Squadron at Presque Isle, Maine. Like Matador and Mace, Snark was rocket-launched; it then levelled off into a high-altitude cruise under turbojet power at just over 600 mph. Its range was 6,300 miles, accuracy of flight was maintained by an astro-inertial guidance system, and the warhead, which could be anything between 5 and 20 megatons, was designed to separate over the target and fall on it in a supersonic trajectory.

Snark, however, was essentially a stop-gap missile, holding the line until the advent of an operational American ICBM. The development of such a weapon had been bedevilled by the prevailing view in the early 1950s that such a weapon was, if not an impossibility, at least too far in the future to bother about, and it was not until 1954 that the USAF decided that the ICBM idea should be seriously considered.

The US Army had been more far-sighted in its approach to missile development, and had the advantage of drawing on the vast rocketry experience of Dr Werner von Braun, head of wartime German V-2 development at Peenemünde, and many of his former staff. In 1950 von Braun and about 150 German engineers were employed at the Redstone Arsenal in Alabama, working alongside several hundred Americans at the US Army's Ordnance Guided Missile Center in a programme to develop a more advanced tactical missile from the V-2. Work was accelerated in 1950, on the outbreak of the Korean War, and the German-American team was given the task of developing a rocket capable of carrying an atomic warhead — which then meant a device weighing some three tons — over a range of 200 miles. It was also to be mobile, and simple enough to be handled by combat troops in the field. The result was the M8 Redstone, a 63-foot missile which was first launched in August 1953; it eventually became operational with US forces in Germany in the summer of 1958 and remained in service until the advent of Pershing in the early 1960s.

Redstone was followed by the first intermediate-range ballistic missile (IRBM), Jupiter, also developed by the Redstone Arsenal team and the first strategic missile in the world to feature an ablative re-entry vehicle — a nose-cone consisting of multiple organic layers, designed to protect the one-megaton warhead from the enormous heat generated by atmospheric re-entry. The system was first tested in September 1956, when a Jupiter-C reached an altitude of 682 miles, and tests of prototypes continued through 1957: by July 1958 there had been 29 total and seven partial successes out of 38 launches.

The 60-foot Jupiter had a range of 1,976 miles and would have provided the US Army, for whom it was originally developed, with an excellent missile system. In 1956, however, the US Secretary of Defense, Charles E. Wilson, declared that no US Army missile should have a range of more than 200 miles, and so the Jupiter programme was handed over to the USAF. Jupiter subsequently equipped the 864th and 865th Strategic Missile Squadrons; each squadron later deployed 30 Jupiter systems to Italy and Turkey under conditions of great secrecy.

By 1959, then, the USAF already had a first-rate IRBM system, and one which had the advantage of being mobile. The irony was that in 1955, as a result of political mismanagement and the often bitter inter-service rivalry that led to the US Army, Air Force and Navy each developing their own missile systems, usually with a wasteful duplication of effort, the USAF was ordered to proceed with the development of an IRBM that was similar in configuration and performance to Jupiter. The contract went to the Douglas Aircraft Corporation, which by prodigious feats of design and engineering delivered the first SM-75 Thor in October 1956, and despite an inauspicious start to the flight test programme — the first four launches ended in failure — the system was declared operational in 1959. The missile itself carried the same warhead over the same range as Jupiter, but unlike the Army missile, it was designed for fixed-base deployment and was consequently far more vulnerable to surprise attack.

From the beginning, it had been the intention of the United States government to deploy Thor missiles in Britain. This proposal was put forward in January 1957 to the British Defence Minister, Duncan Sandys, who was a firm advocate of ballistic missiles and who was deeply involved in the development of Britain's own IRBM, Blue Streak. The latter weapon, however, was not expected to be ready for deployment for some years (in fact it was never to be deployed at all) and the prospect of an interim IRBM deterrent in the form of Thor seemed attractive. Thor, the Americans emphasised, would cost Britain nothing except the funds necessary for site preparation, and to avoid political complications the weapons would be manned by the Royal Air Force, though the warheads would remain under American control.

The proposal was regarded favourably by Britain's new Prime Minister, Harold Macmillan, who saw it as an indication that Anglo-American relations were being restored after a serious deterioration in the autumn of 1956, when British and French forces had jointly invaded the Suez Canal Zone of Egypt. Final agreement on the deployment of Thors in Britain was reached at the Bermuda Conference of March 1957, when Macmillan and Eisenhower met to discuss key issues. On 1 April, Macmillan reported to Parliament that '[the rockets] will be the property of Her Majesty's Government, manned by British troops who will receive their prior training from American experts. The rockets can not be fired by any except the British personnel, but the warhead will be in the control of the United States — which is the law of the United States — and to that extent the Americans have a negative control; but it is absolutely untrue to say that the President and not the British Government will decide when these missiles will be launched and at whom. So long as we rely upon the American warheads, and only so long, that will remain a matter for the two Governments.'

So, despite considerable opposition from various quarters — not least members of the public, who were gradually becoming organised in their expression of disapproval of nuclear weapons — plans for Thor's deployment went ahead, and in February 1958 a joint government agreement was signed. It provided for the Third Air Force to assist in the construction of the Thor sites and deliver the missiles to the RAF, which would maintain and control them, while targeting was to be a matter of joint operational policy, relying on the close liaison established between SAC and RAF Bomber Command.

The plan was for sixty Thors to be supplied to Britain, with twenty re-formed Royal Air Force squadrons operating three missiles each. After its number, each squadron would carry the initials SM (Strategic Missile) — the only RAF squadrons ever to bear this designation.

The first of the designated squadrons, No. 77(SM), was re-formed at Feltwell in Norfolk on 1 September 1958; as yet without missiles, its task was to establish training techniques and procedures with the USAF. Prior to April 1959 the US research and production facilities had been directed mainly towards proving the Thor weapon system at White Sands, New Mexico and Cape Canaveral, Florida, and to setting up the first two missile sites in the United Kingdom. Very little equipment was dedicated to training, and it was not until 16 April 1959 that an RAF crew of No. 98(SM) Squadron, having received formal Integrated Weapon System training, became the first to launch a Thor.

Royal Air Force launch crews, consisting of a General Duties officer (usually a squadron leader) as Launch Control Officer, three aircrew NCOs as Launch Control Console Operators, and three technicians as Missile Maintenance Technicians, were trained at the Douglas Aircraft Company school at Tucson, Arizona. Training comprised missile theory, construction and operation, and an introduction to the necessary ground support equipment. A realistic simulator was used for instruction in countdown sequences, and malfunctions could also be incorporated for emergency training. On graduating from Tucson the crews moved to the home of the USAF's 1st Missile Division at Vandenburg AFB, California, where more detailed training using operational equipment was conducted by the 392nd Missile Training Squadron, assisted by instructors of the Douglas Aircraft Company.

On 19 September 1958 No. 77 Squadron received its first Thor missile, which was flown to Feltwell aboard a USAF C-124 Globemaster, and all subsequent missiles were delivered by this means, along with their ancillary equipment. The missile was still being operationally proven as a weapons system, however, and nearly a year was to elapse before the next batch of RAF squadrons was declared operational with the Thor, on 22 July 1959. These were No. 82 at Shepherd's Grove, Suffolk, No. 104 at Ludford Magna, Lincolnshire, No. 106 at Bardney, also in Lincolnshire, No. 107 at Tuddenham, Suffolk, No. 113 at Mepal, Cambridgeshire, No. 142 at Coleby Grange, Lincolnshire, No. 220 at North Pickenham, Norfolk, and No. 269 at Caistor, Lincolnshire.

Five more RAF Thor units became operational on 1 August 1959, all of them in the East Riding of Yorkshire: No. 98 at Driffield, No. 102 at Full Sutton, No. 150 at Carnaby, No. 226 at Catfoss and No. 240 at Breighton. And it was the end of the year before the six remaining squadrons reached operational status — No. 87 at Hemswell, Lincolnshire, No. 130 at Polebrook, Northamptonshire, No. 144 at North Luffenham, Rutland, No. 218 at Harrington, Northamptonshire, No. 223 at Folkingham, Lincolnshire, and No. 254 at Melton Mowbray, Leicestershire.

Despite the secrecy surrounding the location of the Thors, people in sleepy little towns and villages stretching in an arc from Yorkshire to Suffolk did not take long to realise that, in the space of just a few months, they had jumped into the front line of NATO's nuclear arsenal and would be the first to be hit by an enemy strike if war broke out. Not that the three missiles at each location were much in evidence to the casual onlooker; for much of the time they lay prone and invisible in their shelters, behind heavily guarded perimeters, emerging only for practice countdowns.

Any launch order, simulated or otherwise, had to be authenticated by the RAF and USAF officers at Bomber Command HQ, High Wycombe, where Seventh Air Division's HQ was also located, using a special and highly secret code. Operation of the Thor required a lengthy countdown procedure, so in time of war the system required considerable warning of impending enemy activity; on average, the sequence required something like 105 minutes from receipt of the positive launch order. At that point the RAF Launch Control Officer turned a phase sequence key to initiate a fully automatic sequence of events:

the guidance system was aligned and checked, the shelter moved back and the missile was raised slowly to the upright position, while the liquid propellants were pumped into the missile at a high rate; it had to be pumped out again after a simulated launch.

The liquid-fuel rocket motor was, in fact, the Thor's principal disadvantage, and the time needed to bring the weapon to operational readiness made it vulnerable throughout its career with Bomber Command. Further time would have been needed to fit the nuclear warheads, which were not kept on site but stored with other V-Force weapons under extreme security at Faldingworth, an old wartime airfield near Scampton, Lincolnshire. Such was the secrecy surrounding Faldingworth that, from 1956 to 1980, the airfield was not shown on Ordnance Survey maps. Spare parts for the Thors in the UK were held in the United States; and RAF squadron supply officers could indent direct by radio link for spares and receive them immediately by air, as all the equipment could be carried by the C-124 Globemaster.

Impressive though it was, the Thor deployment in the United Kingdom was nothing more than an interim measure and it terminated in 1963, when the USAF had deployed its first ICBM, the Atlas. At the same time, the RAF's V-Force had reached a new peak of effectiveness with its own deployment of the Blue Steel stand-off weapon, which equipped several squadrons, and Thor squadrons were disbanded, most of them for good.

The Thor deployment has been dealt with at some length here, for two reasons: first because it depended on the full backup of the Third Air Force's mighty logistics machine and on an exceptionally close liaison between the USAF and RAF; and second because it marked the beginning of a new era in the West's deterrent posture. Moreover, the presence of the Thors in the UK was to play its part in persuading the Soviet Union's leaders to deploy their own IRBMs to Cuba in 1962, a decision taken as a result of teething troubles in the early operational deployment of the SS-7 ICBM which temporarily — and unknown to the West — left the USSR dangerously open to attack.

For a time, the United States government had considered the possibility of deploying further IRBMs in France, but by 1959 this was no longer even a vague policy. The redoubtable General de Gaulle had returned to the leadership of his country and showed every sign of embarking on a defensive policy that was separate from that of NATO. He had already withdrawn his fleet from NATO control and had crossed swords with General Lauris Norstad, Supreme Allied Commander Europe, over control of the tactical nuclear weapons deployed on USAF bases in France. The upshot was that, in the summer of 1959, de Gaulle ordered all US nuclear weapons out of France. It was a move that was to have a profound effect on the extent of the USAF's commitment in Britain during the next decade.

F-100 Super Sabres of the 48th Tactical Fighter Wing were deployed to Lakenheath from France in January 1960, beginning an association between the 48th and Britain that still goes on.

The Lockheed C-130 Hercules has been the transport workhorse of the USAF – and many other air forces – for a quarter of a century. The 513th Troop Carrier Wing deployed to Mildenhall from Evreux with these aircraft in 1966.

Grumman SA-16 Albatros amphibians were used by the 67th Air Rescue Squadron at Prestwick in the 1950s and early 1960s.

RF-4C Phantoms of the 10th Tactical Reconnaissance Wing, Alconbury, Huntingdon.
The code letters AR denote the 1st TRS and AS the 30th TRS.

A Northrop F-5E Tiger II of the 527th Tactical Fighter Training Aggressor Squadron, Alconbury. The aircraft has Soviet-style paintwork and numerals.

The ugly but very deadly Fairchild A-10 Thunderbolt II ground attack aircraft. The 81st Fighter-Bomber Wing at Bentwaters and Woodbridge has over 100 of these, and deploys them to forward operating locations in Germany.

6

Crisis in NATO

AN IMMEDIATE CONSEQUENCE of President de Gaulle's veto on American nuclear weapons in France was the removal to England in August 1959 of the 10th Tactical Reconnaissance Wing — not from France, but from Spangdahlem in Germany, to make room for the nuclear-capable fighter-bomber units that would have to be redeployed there. Two RB-66 Tactical Reconnaissance Squadrons, the 1st and the 30th, were relocated at Alconbury, while the 19th and the 42nd went to Bruntingthorpe and Chelveston respectively.

The reshuffle also involved the re-deployment of three tactical fighter wings, all equipped with F-100 Super Sabres: the 49th TFW from Etain to Spangdahlem, the 50th from Toul-Rosières to Hahn and Ramstein, and the 48th to Lakenheath. The impending moves were announced by HQ USAFE at Wiesbaden on 29 December 1959, and the transfer of the flying units began during the first week of the new year.

The Super Sabres of the 48th Tactical Fighter Wing, which had been based at Chaumont, began arriving at Lakenheath on 5 January. It was not a new association with England, for the unit had flown P-47 Thunderbolts from English airfields during the Second World War as the 48th Fighter-Bomber Group before being deactivated in November 1945; reactivated at Chaumont in November' 1952, it had graduated from the F-84G Thunderjet to the F-86F Sabre before re-equipping with the F-100.

While the 48th was stationed in France, the people of Chaumont had petitioned to have the unit named the Statue of Liberty Wing in honour of all the Americans who had died in

99

France during two world wars: the name became official in July 1954, making the 48th the only USAF unit with both a numerical and a descriptive designation. During this period the 48th Fighter-Bomber Group operated as an integral part of the 48th Fighter-Bomber Wing, and when the Group was deactivated for the second time in 1957, with the streamlining of the USAF, its honours and lineage passed to the Wing. In July 1958 the latter was redesignated the 48th Tactical Fighter Wing, and has carried that title ever since.

The growing number of American nuclear weapons deployed in Britain, together with other factors such as the shooting down of USAF U-2 and RB-47 reconnaissance aircraft in the summer of 1960 led to a sharp increase in the activities of the Campaign for Nuclear Disarmament. The likelihood that Britain would be an early target for a Soviet nuclear attack was further increased when, in 1960, construction of a Ballistic Missile Early Warning System (BMEWS) site began with the assistance of Third Air Force at Fylingdales, on the edge of the North Yorkshire Moors; it would come into operation in 1964, and was the third and final link in a BMEWS chain involving other sites in Greenland and Alaska.

The critics of the Fylingdales station pointed out that it extended the warning time available to the United States without conferring a similar benefit on Britain; true, but the British end of the BMEWS chain was a vital link in the efficient functioning of the Western deterrent, in which the RAF's V-Force — geared to scramble in less than two minutes — was indivisible from Strategic Air Command, whose bombers needed considerably longer to get off the ground. In any case, the much-publicised four-minute warning was always something of a myth; before the potential enemy could launch a missile attack there were certain preparations that would have to be made, certain muscles that had to be flexed. The actual warning time might be as little as a few hours; more realistically, it would probably be days or even weeks.

Nevertheless, the USAF presence in Britain had attracted sufficient adverse publicity to persuade the Committee of 100 (the leadership of CND) that the time had come to take direct action, and in November 1961, in the wake of an earlier series of passive protests, the Committee announced that its supporters would attempt to immobilise the US air bases at Wethersfield and Brize Norton, infiltrate Third AF HQ at Ruislip and organise civil disobedience at Bristol, Cardiff, Manchester and York.

The Committee claimed that some of its members had already succeeded in penetrating Wethersfield, driving around the perimeter track unchallenged and drawing a sketch map of the installations, but the new plan was pre-empted when, forty-eight hours before the demonstrations were due to take place, Special Branch officers swooped on the headquarters and homes of members of the Committee of 100, seizing hundreds of documents. At the same time, police issued stern warnings that the Americans had every right to open fire on intruders, par-ticularly those who entered sensitive areas; the Americans for their part quietly stepped up their security patrols and strengthened the perimeter fencing at Wethersfield, which — in contrast to the twelve-foot barbed-wire fence at Brize Norton — consisted of only three wire strands for much of its six-mile length. On this occasion the demonstrators were successfully kept at arm's length, but the activities of the CND were hence-forth to remain a very sharp thorn in Third Air Force's side.

The summer of 1962 saw the cessation of operational flying at three USAF bases following another change in operational requirements. At Sculthorpe, the 47th Bomb Wing deactivated on 22 June 1962 and the airfield became a standby base. Chelveston also became a reserve airfield in August with the departure of the RB-66s of the 42nd TRS, while Brunt-ingthorpe was abandoned in September. Another change involved the move late in 1962 of Third Air Force HQ from Ruislip to its present location at Mildenhall.

In October 1962, as a result of the Cuban missile crisis, both Strategic Air Command units based in the UK and the RAF's V-Force stood alert for a period of three days until the Russians backed down in the face of President Kennedy's ultimatum and confirmed that they would begin dismantling the IRBMs they had deployed in Cuba. SAC and V-Force units alike were unobtrusively brought up to a high degree of readiness; civilian personnel on the bases were sent home, the bases themselves sealed off from the outside and their perimeters secured by armed patrols, while the V-Bombers and B-47s stood armed and combat-ready. At no time during the alert, however, did British or American aircraft fly from UK bases with armed weapons on board.

In the early weeks of 1963, following the news that the ageing B-47 Stratojet was to be phased out of the bomber role, there were rumours that the Seventh Air Division's bomber bases in the UK were soon to close. This was denied by a Seventh AD spokesman at High Wycombe in February, only to be replaced by a new rumour that the B-47s were to be replaced by a radical new bomber, the Convair B-58 Hustler, the first supersonic bomber to enter service with the USAF. It had, in fact, been anticipated that the Hustler would replace the B-47 in SAC's medium bomber force, but in the event only enough aircraft were built to equip six squadrons in two wings, the 43rd and 305th.

Individual B-58s did visit Brize Norton and Greenham Common from October 1963; before that, B-58s had visited Britain briefly in the course of record-breaking flights. On 16 October 1962, for example, one aircraft flew non-stop across the North Pole from Tokyo to London in eight hours thirty-five minutes at an average speed of 938 mph, being refuelled in flight five times. But the Hustler's operational career was relatively short-lived, and the type was withdrawn from SAC service in 1968.

Despite conflicting rumours, it was becoming increasingly clear in the spring of 1963 that Strategic Air Command's mission in the United Kingdom was coming to an end. This was confirmed by Seventh Air Division in April, although it was emphasised that there would be no closure of the SAC bases at Greenham Common, Fairford, Upper Heyford and Brize Norton until 1964.

On 17 April 1963 General Truman H. Landon, Commander-in-Chief of the United States Air Forces in Europe, announced that the command structure of USAFE was being realigned to reduce manpower. The tactical fighter wings that had been withdrawn from France in 1960, and which had remained under the operational control of the Seventeenth Air

Force in Germany, would now come under the command of the Third Air Force, though the change, which was to be completed by October 1963, was purely administrative and would not involve the movement of aircraft or personnel. Third Air Force was also to assume operational control of the tactical and reconnaissance units still in France, leaving Seventeenth AF responsible for Germany.

In October 1963 the USAF and US Army participated jointly in a massive exercise called Operation Big Lift, which involved airlifting the entire Second Armored Division from Fort Hood, Texas, to Germany in sixty hours. Troops began to board C-124s and C-135s in Texas on October 22, while other Military Air Transport Service aircraft began collecting their support equipment and that of four USAF fighter squadrons involved in the exercise. The long-range transports flew directly to Germany, while smaller aircraft staged via Bermuda, Greenland and the Azores, and all 15,000 men and 450 tons of equipment were delivered to Rhein-Main AFB, Sembach AFB and Ramstein AFB and were in action within the planned sixty hours.

This exercise preceded an announcement later that month that substantial cuts were to be made in the USAF establishment in Britain over the following two years. The Tactical Air Division's bases were to be handed back to the Air Ministry in the summer of 1964, and the reductions would involve about ten per cent of the USAF personnel then stationed in Britain, or about 2,500 men.

On 8 November it was confirmed that the SAC bases to be affected would be Fairford and Greenham Common. Their closure would involve the withdrawal of nineteen B-47s and twenty-two supporting flight-refuelling tanker aircraft, most of them based at Sculthorpe with the 420th Air Refuelling Squadron. Fairford was returned to MoD control in June 1964 and subsequently became the home of C Flight of the RAF's Central Flying School until September 1966, when it was taken over by Transport Command. Greenham Common reverted to MoD control on 1 July 1964.

The remaining Reflex Alert B-47 detachments, with their supporting tankers, were now concentrated at Brize Norton and Upper Heyford, but in the spring of 1965 Strategic Air Command terminated all its bomber operations in Britain and Brize Norton was taken over by the MoD on 1 April. The last Stratojet to leave Britain was a B-47E of the 380th Bomb Wing, which took off from Brize Norton on 3 April. Upper Heyford, however, remained under American control as a Dispersed Operating Base under the care of the 7514th Combat Support Group.

Not long afterwards, American air defence policy within the framework of European NATO was turned upside down by a sudden — but hardly unexpected — move on the part of the French. Ever since 1958 President de Gaulle had been steadily reducing the French commitment to NATO, and by early 1966 the American embassy in Paris was aware that the French government was preparing a request for changes in the various Franco-American agreements on US bases and troops in France. De Gaulle took a deliberately misleading line, telling the US ambassador that there would be no precipitate action on France's part, but on 22 February he warned that he would like all NATO headquarters and foreign troops out of France by the end of the first twenty-year period of the NATO treaty, in other words by April 1969.

A fortnight later, on 7 March, de Gaulle delivered his bombshell in a personal letter to President Lyndon Johnson and the heads of government of Britain, Canada, Federal Germany and Italy. It read:

> In three years our Atlantic Alliance will complete its first term. I am anxious to tell you that France appreciates the extent to which the solidarity of defence thus established between fifteen free peoples of the West contributes to assuring their security, and especially what essential role the United States plays in this respect. Accordingly France intends from now on to remain party to the treaty signed at Washington on 4 April 1949. This means that, except in the event of developments which might occur in the course of the next three years to change the fundamental factors of East--West relations, she will be, in 1969 and thereafter, determined, even as today to fight at the side of her allies in case one of them will be the object of unprovoked aggression.

However, France considers the changes which have taken place or are in the process of occurring since 1949 in Europe, Asia and elsewhere, as well as the evolution of her own situation and her own forces, no longer justify insofar as that concerns her the arrangements of a military nature adopted after the conclusion of the alliance, whether in common under the form of multilateral conventions or whether by special agreement between the French Government and the American Government.

It is for this reason that France proposes to recover the entire exercise of her sovereignty over her territory, presently impaired by the permanent presence of allied military elements or by constant utilization which is made of her air space, to terminate her participation in the 'integrated' commands and no longer places her forces at the disposal of NATO. . .

De Gaulle's message was quite clear. France now possessed her own tactical nuclear weapons and the aircraft, as advanced as any in the world, to deliver them; her first missile-armed nuclear submarines were being built; she would eventually have her own IRBMs; and the size of her conventional forces was increasing. France, in other words, could look after herself. But there was something else; de Gaulle was about to visit the Soviet Union, and he undoubtedly saw France's abrogation of her NATO commitments as a powerful lever in his forthcoming negotiations with Russia's leaders — perhaps the preliminary to a major shift in Soviet foreign policy for which he could claim much credit.

At the end of March the NATO Allies were informed that all French officers would be withdrawn from Supreme Headquarters Allied Powers Europe (SHAPE) and from other NATO commands too. On 1 April all French forces in Germany and elsewhere would cease to be under NATO command, and the Allies were given one year from that date to remove SHAPE and all other NATO headquarters, bases, troops and storage facilities from French territory.

At this time USAFE still had a considerable concentration of air power in northern France, with units based at Chaumont,

Dreux, Evreux-Fauville, Laon, Etain, Chambley, Toul-Rosières, Phalsbourg and Châteauroux — although of course none of the remaining units was nuclear-equipped; the majority, in fact, were transport and reconnaissance units. With the launching of Operation Freloc — French Relocation of Assets — in the summer of 1966, these units were redeployed to bases in Britain, Federal Germany and the Netherlands. Britain's share in the reshuffle was two additional USAF wings, the 513th Troop Carrier Wing from Evreux and the 66th Tactical Reconnaissance Wing from Laon. The latter, equipped with RF-101C Voodoos, repositioned at Upper Heyford on 1 September 1966; the 513th TCW, with C-130 Hercules transports, went to Mildenhall along with the EC-135s of Silk Purse Control, the European Command's airborne command post facility. Another unit, the Military Airlift Command's 322nd Air Division HQ, was moved from Châteauroux to High Wycombe, but was later relocated at Rhein-Main AFB in Germany.

Meanwhile, some of the Third Air Force's resident units in the United Kingdom had benefited from a re-equipment programme. On 12 May 1965 two McDonnell RF-4C Phantoms touched down at Alconbury after a 5,750-mile non-stop flight lasting eight hours forty minutes from North Carolina. The first of the two aircraft was piloted by Colonel deWitt S. Spain, commander of the 10th Tactical Reconnaissance Wing, and its arrival at Alconbury heralded the beginning of the 10th TRW's conversion to the new type.

The RF-4C Phantom, which still equipped the 10th TRW in 1986, was the first all-weather, day and night tactical reconnaissance aircraft on the USAF's inventory. Carrying a crew of two — a pilot and systems operator — the aircraft is powered by two General Electric J79 turbojets developing over 34,000 pounds of thrust with afterburning. Thanks to high lift devices and boundary layer control it can fly at speeds as low as 150 mph, leading and trailing edge flaps providing increased lift at the high angles of attack required for sustained low-speed flying. At the other end of the scale, the RF-4C has an over-the-target dash speed of more than 1,600 mph and can reach a maximum altitude of over 50,000 feet in just over six minutes from the start of its take-off roll.

For its reconnaissance mission the RF-4C carries forward-looking radar and optical and infrared sensor systems. The optical sensors incorporate high- and low-altitude panoramic cameras, forward-, vertical- and side-mounted framing cameras and high-altitude mapping cameras. The infrared sensors produce detailed maps from variable altitudes and in any weather conditions.

The reconnaissance data gathered during operations, depending on the urgency attached to it, can be disseminated through air-to-ground high frequency communication for the rapid deployment of tactical aircraft — known as direct reconnaissance reporting — or recorded on film for analysis on the ground. At the end of a mission the film shot by the RF-4C is rushed to the Photographic Processing and Interpretation Facility (PPIF), a self-contained complex at Alconbury.

Within thirty minutes of engine shutdown the film must be processed and the imagery interpreter must confirm the mission report (MISREP) made by the aircrew; the interpreter then makes a detailed readout of the mission film, and the completed reports, negatives, maps and prints must be ready for forwarding to the user no later than four hours after engine shutdown. Reports are sent electronically, while the prints and negatives are forwarded by aircraft, and the information obtained from the interpreter reports can be used to determine priorities of targets, approaches to targets, bomb damage assessment, enemy resources and battle situations.

On 4 October 1965 the 81st Tactical Fighter Wing at Bentwaters also received its first Phantom. This was the F-4C version, developed for close support and ground attack with Tactical Air Command and able to carry the formidable load of up to 16,000 pounds of tactical nuclear or conventional stores. Conversion of the 81st TFW's squadrons at Bentwaters and Woodbridge was completed by April 1966; in April 1969 the 78th TFS at Woodbridge received the F-4D Phantom, basically an F-4C with improved avionics.

The news of their impending withdrawal from France came as a complete shock to many USAF personnel stationed there; the first most of them knew about the order was an announcement by Robert McNamara, the United States Defense

Secretary. Once the news broke, however, they accepted it philosophically. Tactically, USAFE's NATO commitment was not hindered; in fact, there was a school of thought that claimed there would be an increase in efficiency following the move, since de Gaulle would cease to be a thorn in NATO's side. There were social benefits, too: as one US airman put it, 'It is sad that the French take this attitude. I think that most of us feel this way, but Britain is generally regarded as a better posting — I mean to say, you speak American, so it's easier!'

The move to Britain involved some 8,000 Air Force personnel and their dependents. Because the move was announced at short notice careful plans were made to avoid swamping the accommodation available in areas around the air bases. A sudden influx could inflate property prices and cause a lot of resentment among local residents — an old chestnut that had burned the Americans' fingers on more than one occasion in the past. So servicemen whose three-year overseas tour was nearly completed were returned to the United States, while the 2,000 married men who were moving to England were not allowed to bring their families with them immediately. 'They must find a home first and produce the lease or contract for it and only then can their families join them,' said a Third Air Force spokesman in September 1966. 'Otherwise hotels would be booked up to the ceiling and it would be an impossible situation.'

Once the USAF's impressive logistics organisation had moved into full stride Operation Freloc moved smoothly enough. The day after it began, Hercules transports of the 513th Troop Carrier Wing were already going about their NATO business from Mildenhall, and within a few days eighteen of the Wing's aircraft had departed for an exercise in Greece.

Admittedly, USAF personnel who found themselves posted to Britain in the late 1960s had little to complain about. In off-base rented accommodation they got on well enough with their English neighbours, and many integrated completely with the local community. But these were families; in other areas, there were inevitable problems, and they usually concerned the category of airman known as Grade B Bachelors — married men separated from their wives by service.

In 1968 life for such a man in Britain seemed to have a lot to offer. Petrol from the base ration cost two shillings a gallon, cigarettes were seven shillings and sixpence a hundred from the PX, the US Forces Exchange Shop, hard liquor was fifteen shillings a quart, and he could buy a magnum of champagne for 25 shillings. He could buy an English sports car free of tax, and if he owned it for more than six months he could ship it back to the US free of federal and state taxes and sell it at a handsome profit.

In 1969, however, the US government introduced Operation Goldflow, which was designed to slow down the dollar drain by curbing the off-base spending of US servicemen overseas. Its immediate result was to make the life of a bachelor airman — or an airman separated from his wife and family — introspective and forcibly self-contained. He could spend his money on base, where Club life was well organised but tedious after a time, or he could try to get off base into the nearest town, an activity often limited by the fact that, after the government clampdown in spending, few young GIs could afford a car.

A combination of boredom and frustration led, over the years, to a number of much-publicised breakdowns among USAF personnel serving in Britain. One of the earliest occurred in August 1955, when a young Negro GI, 21-year-old Napoleon Green, who was awaiting trial at Manston, went berserk and broke into the armoury, where he armed himself with a revolver and rifle. In the space of a couple of hours he shot and killed a USAF Master Sergeant, an airman and an RAF police corporal and wounded three other GIs and six British civilians by shooting indiscriminately at passing cars. A Hollywood-style chase, in which he forced another sergeant to drive him to Broadstairs at gunpoint, ended with his suicide at Rocky Beach Pools.

There were three serious incidents in 1958, the first in June when a mechanic who considered himself a frustrated pilot climbed at night into the cockpit of an 85th Bombardment Squadron B-45 Tornado and tried to take off, only to smash himself and the aircraft to pieces almost immediately on the main London-Edinburgh railway line at Wood Walton. Then, in October, Master Sergeant Leander Cunningham, one of six senior nuclear weapons technicians, locked himself for eight hours in a weapons store at Sculthorpe and threatened to detonate an atomic warhead with his revolver before shooting himself. In the event he gave himself up; the safety precautions described earlier made his threat an empty one, though he could certainly have caused a conventional HE explosion. A few days later, Technical Sergeant James Dobbs left Brize Norton, where he was a cashier, with a revolver, several rounds of ammunition and 4,000 dollars, which he blew in a four-day spending spree before surrendering to a surprised London bobby.

Murder trials involving US personnel always attracted a great deal of publicity, partly because of the amount of psychiatric evidence offered and partly because the outcome often left both American and English lawyers in a state of confusion. In one celebrated case, high-living Master Sergeant Marcus Marymont went to the stockade at Fort Leavenworth for the rest of his life for poisoning his wife so that he could marry his English mistress, Mrs Cynthia Taylor. What startled English jurists was the additional charge at his Denham court martial of having 'wrongful intercourse' with Mrs Taylor.

American military jurists were equally astonished when another high-spender, Staff Sergeant Willis Boshears, a Grade B Bachelor at the time, was acquitted at Essex Assizes in 1961 of murdering his English girlfriend, twenty-year-old Jean Constable, as she slept with him on a mattress after a party. Boshears pleaded that he must have strangled her while he was asleep and an English jury found him not guilty. He died in a car crash in the USA a few years later.

In May 1969 a ground staff NCO at Mildenhall, Sergeant Paul Meyer — another Grade B Bachelor — made an unauthorised take-off in a C-130 Hercules of the 513th TCW and disappeared along with the aircraft. Its wreckage was later found drifting in the English Channel thirty miles south of Bournemouth: according to the Air Force, Meyer took the aircraft because of a combination of 'lovesickness and too much alcohol'. His wife Jane, at her home in Poquoson, Virginia, professed herself mystified by his action.

The night he stole the Hercules, Meyer got drunk at a party in the home of Mrs Christine Allan, in Heathersetway, Red Lodge, near Mildenhall base. Another guest, Mrs Dawn Full-wood, told reporters: 'I was at the party, and I want to make it clear that there was no orgy going on or anything like that. There was a bit of dancing to records and, of course, quite a lot of hard drinking by the Americans. Sergeant Meyer was very moody and quiet, but he gave no impression that he was likely to do anything desperate.'

But neighbour Mrs Ayla Underwood talked about what happened after Meyer left the party and ran drunkenly through back yards and over car-port roofs. She said: 'I was in bed when there was a terrific hammering at the door. Meyer was outside. He asked if he could come inside. I awakened my husband from bed, and Meyer ran away behind a tree. While I was phoning the police Meyer came back. He banged so hard on the window my husband let him in. Immediately, he became very rational and friendly. He had my little boy's blue jeans stuck in his pants. They had been hanging on the line outside.'

Air Force officials said that when Meyer took off he flew over the Thames Estuary east of London, then passed over Brighton at about 16,000 feet. Over the Channel he headed for Le Havre, but doubled back towards Weymouth before vanishing. The extraordinary thing about the incident was that, just before he crashed, Meyer made a transmission over the aircraft's radio on a channel that was tuned directly to Langley AFB in Virginia, his previous home base. His wife lived there, and he was apparently trying to call her.

As a result of the Meyer incident, the 513th Wing chained its transport aircraft to the ground to stop homesick airmen steal-ing them. But the scheme had a drawback — pilots and ground crew had to trudge to the control tower for the keys, forms had to be filled in triplicate and signatures obtained. Then someone wanted to know what would happen in an emergency if the aircraft had to be moved in a hurry, and after three weeks the scheme was quietly dropped.

The Vietnam War brought a new set of social problems. Drug offences among US servicemen in Britain and elsewhere rose sharply and there was a growing involvement with anti-war movements, particularly among young short-service air-men. It was a problem that seriously concerned the USAF, especially as some of the peace movements had strong com-munist connections and were apparently fronts for more sinis-ter organisations. In 1970 a group of US airmen in Britain formed an organisation named PEACE (People Emerging Against Corrupt Establishments) which eventually had about 200 active members and some 4,000 sympathisers, and on Whit Monday 1971 the 200 activists — drawn from nine USAF and US Navy bases throughout Britain — attended a rally in Hyde Park, along with a substantial gathering of British anti-war protestors, and subsequently handed petitions bearing 900 signatures to the US Embassy.

The proceedings were monitored by agents of the OSI — the Office of Special Investigations, the American forces' equiv-alent of the FBI — and as a result a number of the personnel involved became subject to investigation. At both Mildenhall and Upper Heyford USAF spokesmen said that it had been made clear to the men well before the approach to the embassy that the PEACE rally would be regarded as a demonstration, and that channels had been set up at the USAF bases for individuals to petition their officers by legal means. It was further claimed that the protestors had been distributing sub-versive literature on some bases, which contravened all manner of regulations.

One of the men involved was Captain Thomas Culver, a thirty-two-year-old USAF lawyer at Lakenheath: since he was an officer, the USAF decided to make an example of him, and he was brought before a court martial charged with taking part in a demonstration. Small groups of PEACE supporters daily attended Culver's court martial, which was held at Lakenheath, and the proceedings provoked a bitter reaction against the system. The supporters, in contrast to the crisp, all-American look of most USAF airmen, turned up at the hear-ings with hair long, shoes dirty, and wearing multi-coloured clothes that often featured T-shirts with clenched fist emblems across the chest. They were fond of quoting Regulation 39/12, which set in motion the administrative discharge machinery by which the Air Force got rid of 'undesirables'. One protestor, a

22-year-old black airman called Stan Miser, told reporters bitterly: 'The US Air Force has two reactions to guys who want to express opinions. One, they try to change them, and thereby the opinions. Two, if they can't do that, they whip you out. And I'm due to be shipped out any time now.' He was.

The trial was bizarre. One of the witnesses for the prosecution, Sergeant Joseph B. Wilson, who had been acting as an undercover agent for OSI during the Whit Monday rally, admitted under cross-examination that he had supplied photographs to the British Press. Questioned about his own beliefs, he startled defence and prosecution lawyers alike by telling them that he was a witch and had been an adherent of the 'Old Religion' for nine years. The court martial ended with Culver being reprimanded and fined $1,000.

A few days later, in defiance of a ban, about thirty GIs — all wearing dark glasses and floppy hats to disguise their identities — turned up at Grosvenor Square to hand in yet another petition to the US Embassy. PEACE organisers had expected at least 500 to turn out, so it was all a bit of a letdown. In the end, the movement died a natural death; the end of the war in Vietnam left nothing to protest about, and the prime movers of PEACE had, in service parlance, been quietly shuffled sideways.

These incidents, which naturally attracted a great deal of publicity in the popular media, involved only a tiny proportion of the total USAF personnel stationed in Britain and gave a completely false impression of the USAF's professionalism. And there was little doubt that by 1971 the Third Air Force had reached a higher standard of competence than ever before, partly because its ranks now included men who had served combat tours in Vietnam, and partly because it had begun to receive equipment that was technically more advanced than any in the world.

On 1 April 1970 the 66th Tactical Reconnaissance Wing — by then operating a mix of Voodoos and RF-4Cs — was deactivated at Upper Heyford, and in the months that followed extensive modifications were carried out on the base, turning it into the largest of its kind in Europe. The reason for all the activity became apparent when, following the arrival of the 20th Tactical Fighter Wing HQ from Wethersfield, two F-111 swing-wing fighter-bombers touched down at the Oxfordshire base.

7

The Interdictors

THE FIRST PAIR of General Dynamics F-111E tactical fighter-bombers that flew into Upper Heyford on 12 September 1970 brought a completely new dimension to the Third Air Force's already considerable striking power. At last the NATO air forces in Europe had an aircraft that was capable of delivering either nuclear or conventional weapons to targets deep inside Warsaw Pact territory at night and in all weathers; an aircraft whose advanced electronic systems and low-level penetration capability greatly enhanced its chances of survival in a hostile environment thick with surface-to-air missiles and anti-aircraft artillery.

Admittedly, the F-111's baptism of fire in Vietnam two years earlier had ended inauspiciously with the loss of three of the six aircraft that had been sent out for combat evaluation to Takhli Air Base, Thailand, in an operation code-named Combat Lancer. Two of the aircraft had gone missing without trace, but the third had come down in friendly territory and the crew had been picked up; they told how the aircraft had suddenly gone out of control, and a subsequent examination of the wreckage revealed that a control rod had suffered metal fatigue at a welded joint. All F-111s were grounded while this problem and another involving structural failure of the wing pivots were sorted out, and when the F-111 went back to Vietnam in 1972, shortly before the close of that unhappy war, it performed outstandingly against targets that were defended by the heaviest anti-aircraft concentration the world had ever seen.

With one exception, the F-111 is the most sophisticated interdictor in the world. The exception is the Tornado, developed jointly by Britain, West Germany and Italy and in service with the air forces of those three countries since 1982; but by then the F-111 had been in service with the USAF for fifteen years, and it is still going strong.

Years ahead of its time it incorporated many novel design features, such as its zero-speed, zero-altitude emergency escape module. The F-111's two-man crew sit side by side in an air-conditioned and pressurised cabin that forms part of the module; the portion of the canopy over each seat is hinged on the aircraft centreline and opens upwards. The emergency escape procedure, which can also be initiated when the aircraft is under water, calls for both crew members to remain in the module cabin section, which is boosted away from the aircraft by a 40,000-pound thrust rocket motor and lowered to the ground by parachute. Air bags cushion the impact on land and form flotation gear in the event of an over-water escape, while the whole capsule forms a survival shelter.

The self-contained escape module provides an unprecedented degree of crew comfort; the absence of ejection seats means that there is no complex strapping-in process, all knobs, switches and keyboards are readily to hand, and there is plenty of stowage space for maps and other documents. The only real drawback is the poor pilot visibility; the pilot must rely on his systems to alert him to any threat approaching from a sixty degree cone to the rear, and on his Weapon System Officer's eyes to check the sky to starboard. Since the F-111's primary mission is low-level interdiction at night or in bad weather, however, this is not a serious shortcoming, as the aircraft depends on jamming and deception for its survival.

The re-equipment of the 20th Tactical Fighter Wing with its full complement of seventy-two F-111Es was completed by the summer of 1971, and the inhabitants of Oxfordshire were quickly getting used to the large and noisy swing-wing jets overhead. Keen aircraft spotters could also distinguish the squadron to which a particular aircraft belonged, because each of the 20th's three Tactical Fighter Squadrons carried a different colour on the rear warning radar antenna on top of the fin: blue for the 55th, red for the 77th and yellow for the 79th. The fins carried different code letters, too — JR for the 79th, JS for the 55th and JT for the 77th — but this practice was later dropped and all Upper Heyford F-111s were given the tailcode UH.

The F-111 was a far cry from the F-100s that had previously equipped the 20th. Its performance was startling; at high level the aircraft's maximum speed was in the region of Mach 2.5 — two and a half times the speed of sound — and a red warning light instructed the pilot to throttle back if the aircraft approached the limiting Mach number, otherwise friction would heat the skin to a degree where structural failure might occur. With wings swept at forty-five degrees the aircraft nosed through Mach 1 effortlessly, and maximum speed was reached with them fully swept at seventy-two and a half degrees. The climb was spectacular, too: under the combined 36,000-pound thrust of its two Pratt & Whitney TF30 turbofan engines it was quite capable of reaching Mach 2 in the climb, which — for reasons of fuel conservation as well as to protect the ears of the citizens of Oxfordshire — nobody wished to happen.

With the arrival of their first aircraft the crews of the 20th — whose conversion course had been unusual in having taken place in the United Kingdom rather than in the United States — embarked on a period of intensive training, and soon the needle-nosed F-111s became a regular sight as they streaked along the low-level training routes that intersect the remoter areas of the British Isles.

Low-level training was — and remains — the primary requirement, for without it no interdictor could survive in a hostile environment. Interdiction involves getting right down on the deck, under the probing radar beams and the launch envelopes of the deadly SAM missiles; it also means obliterating a target the crew might never see except on their radar displays in the first pass after a low-level flight of several hundred miles. That's why F-111s, Tornados and other hot military hardware scream up and down beautiful Lakeland valleys and over Scottish glens, throwing the inhabitants of remote villages into a frenzy; one day, they might be called upon to do the same thing through other, less friendly valleys, in deadly earnest. If they wait until then to start learning the necessary tactics and skills, it will be too late.

To carry out its primary task of low-level penetration the F-111 has an astonishing array of electronic equipment. At the heart of it all is a CP-2A digital computer, which processes all the information from the aircraft's systems and presents it to the crew in intelligible form. Then there is a General Electric APQ-113 J-band multi-mode radar providing accurate air to ground navigation, ranging and weapon delivery facilities; in an air-to-air role it can track and scan hostile targets and control the aiming and launch of Sidewinder air-to-air missiles.

One of the most vital items of equipment is the Texas Instruments APQ-110 terrain-following radar, which is fully automatic and enables the aircraft to follow the contours of the ground at a height of 200 feet without the pilot touching the controls. With TFR operating the F-111 can skim over the ground at Mach 1.2 — one and two-tenths times the speed of sound. What happens is that the TF antenna nods up and down, scanning a narrow sector ahead of the aircraft to determine the height of the approaching terrain. This information is processed by the computer and transmitted to the aircraft flight control system, which raises or lowers the nose as necessary.

The aircraft's track across the ground is determined by the navigational computers; all the pilot has to do is operate the throttles to compensate for any increase or decrease in speed and, in conjunction with the Weapon Systems Officer, monitor the TFR constantly to make sure that everything is working properly. At such times the atmosphere on board becomes very tense, especially over mountainous terrain at night, when all the F-111 crew can see is the dark grey of the inside of a cloud, punctuated by the red flashes of the aircraft's rotating beacon. It is small wonder that a qualified pilot needs a full year's training before he is fully conversant with the F-111's systems and can be declared ready to fly operational missions.

For an F-111 crew, a training sortie is a full day's work. First there is a lengthy briefing, involving such factors as selecting the best low-level route to the target, and even when the crew arrive at their aircraft they have to go through a massive checklist of necessary items for another hour or so before they can take off.

Much of this time is spent in checking out the WSO's

equipment, which includes a combined radar and projected map display, ground mapping radar, stores management system for selecting what weapons are to be used and when, weapon-aiming mode selector, passive radar warning receiver and an active electronic countermeasures system. The aircraft's planned route is entered into the inertial navigation system by means of a computer keyboard; information includes flight time to turning-points, navigational checks on route — known as waypoints — and so on.

While the pilot monitors the terrain-following radar displaying the aircraft's low-level flight path, the WSO monitors the progress of the flight on his ground-mapping radar and carries out radar position fixes and weapon aiming; either crew member can update the present position stored in the central computer. Thanks to the stores management system, the navigator can assign weapons to a particular target before flight, and when a release signal is received from the main computer the stores management system automatically drops the correct weapons.

Once the F-111's manufacturers had sorted out its early technical problems, its performance in Vietnam was astonishing. During the closing weeks of 1972, during Operation Linebacker II, F-111s of the 429th and 430th Tactical Fighter Squadrons, operating out of Takhli, hit their targets time after time in conditions when no other aircraft could fly. They entered the target area as low down as their TFR would permit, because the North Vietnamese defences were terrifying: attacking crews had to fly through terrain that was stiff with surveillance radars on every piece of high ground, under a night sky bright with anti-aircraft fire and SAM missile salvos — one F-111 crew reported fifty missile launches as they passed through the target area near Hanoi. But they succeeded in their mission, and the first indication the North Vietnamese usually had of an F-111 in the vicinity was when its bombs started exploding around their ears, often in weather so bad that the enemy had believed no attack was possible.

In England, the second unit to receive F-111s after the 20th TFW was the 48th Tactical Fighter Wing, which exchanged its F-4D Phantoms for F-111Fs in March 1977. Eighty-four aircraft were eventually involved, so with their arrival at Lakenheath the F-111 force's strength in the United Kingdom rose to 156 aircraft in total.

The two F-111 wings gave a massive boost to NATO's long-range theatre strike force in Europe, their primary roles being theatre nuclear strike, conventional interdiction, and counter-air attack; secondary roles are close air support, air defence suppression and maritime air support. For these roles the F-111 carries a formidable array of weapons, including two tactical nuclear weapons, two 2,000-pound conventional high explosive bombs or an M61 cannon in the internal weapons bay, or up to about 14,000 pounds of bombs or missiles on its wing pylons.

The F-111 has shown itself to be highly adaptable to advanced weapon-delivery systems. Between September 1977 and August 1978 it carried out a series of trials with Pave Tack, a self-contained pod incorporating a laser designator and rangefinder and forward-looking infrared equipment for use with guided weapons such as the Maverick missile; Pave Tack has equipped the F-111Fs of the 48th TFW at Lakenheath since 1982. Tests with Pave Tack and Maverick involved three launches and resulted in two direct hits; in the third case the missile missed the target through a fault in its TV guidance system.

Other Pave Tack trials were carried out with laser-guided bombs; these resulted in practically 100 per cent direct hits, and tests with unguided bombs showed delivery accuracies roughly twice those attainable by radar. The Pave Tack pod is stowed inside the F-111's weapons bay in a special cradle and is completely recessed inside the bay when not in use, rotating through 180 degrees in five seconds to expose the gimballed sensor head when the system is activated. Once exposed, the sensor head can be rotated to cover the complete lower hemisphere, and provides a stable platform for the forward-looking infrared seeker, the laser designator and rangefinder. The stabilised infrared image, together with range information, is presented to the Weapon Systems Operator on a special display.

On a low-level run towards the target the primary display

shows a radar ground map which enables major course corrections to be made. At just under four miles from the target Pave Tack is activated by the WSO to provide more accurate steering information and the infrared image appears on the display. After selecting the correct infrared field of view the WSO centres a reticle on the target and fires the laser, which is kept on target by the aircraft's inertial navigation system even when the F-111 is jinking to avoid ground fire, and the WSO uses a hand controller for fine tuning of the laser line of sight. With the laser illuminating the target the F-111's central computer initiates a pull-up and automatically releases the weapons at the optimum point for an accurate toss-delivery attack; as the aircraft turns away from the target Pave Tack's sensor head rotates so that it continues to provide target illumination until bomb impact. The pod is then retracted and the aircraft, having pulled round hard and dived back to low level, accelerates to supersonic speed for its escape from the target area.

Since its arrival in the UK the USAF's F-111 force has demonstrated its abilities in numerous realistic combat exercises. Although they form only ten per cent of the USAF's tactical fighter force in Europe, their effectiveness is largely unimpaired when the weather deteriorates. In one NATO Reforger exercise in Europe, F-111s were scheduled to complete 194 sorties, thirty per cent of the total number of missions to be flown by US tactical fighters. In the event, bad weather cut the number of F-111 sorties to 166, but this represented 64 per cent of the actual missions flown by all aircraft, and no fewer than 145 of the F-111 sorties were judged to have hit their targets — a staggering 86 per cent of the successful missions flown by all US fighters involved.

During training F-111 crews either fly at low level all the way to the target and back, or, over longer distances, adopt the hi-lo-hi formula. A typical training sortie might involve an hour of high-level cruise, half an hour of low-level practice with fifteen minutes or so spent in dropping practice bombs or illuminating targets by radar, and high-level cruise back to base. For the crews, it is an exhilarating business. As one crew member put it, 'Cruising at eight miles a minute, 500 feet off the ground, is exciting and beautiful. You're low enough to get a really good look at the countryside, and in the United Kingdom that's rugged coastline, lakes, mountains and castles. After a while, 500 feet seems quite high — you can get quite comfortable there, at least in daylight.'

Even with the introduction of advanced combat aircraft such as the Tornado and the F-15E Eagle, the F-111 — or Aardvark, as it is unofficially known — remains the only NATO tactical fighter that is capable of reaching one-third of the likely Warsaw Pact targets in central Europe. Details of what those targets are likely to be are, of course, highly classified, but training flights are known to take the UK-based F-111s as far afield as the Baltic and the Adriatic, and from both these positions the aircraft could strike deep into Warsaw Pact territory.

In a European war scenario it is logical to assume that while Tornados and Buccaneers of Royal Air Force Strike Command carried out attacks on ports, airfields, radar complexes and missile sites in the Soviet Arctic — at Murmansk and Archangelsk, for example — as well as maintaining an air offensive against units of the Soviet Northern and Baltic Fleets, the F-111 strike force would penetrate Warsaw Pact territory from north and south to hit command and communications centres, supply bases, road and rail links, fuel depots and possibly oilfield installations.

The radius of action of an F-111 carrying various weapon and fuel loads is secret, but is thought to be about 1,000 nautical miles with a 6,000-pound war load. This means that an F-111 in this configuration could fly at high level across the 'neck' of Denmark, descend to low level at a turning point over the Baltic, and penetrate Russian territory as far as Minsk. Alternatively, flying directly across central Europe, F-111s could cover the whole of Czechoslovakia or Poland — and from advanced NATO bases on Cyprus or in Turkey its combat radius would enable it to strike at targets in Russia's vital Caucasian oilfields.

The public — and, for that matter, the potential enemy — received a remarkable insight into the F-111's capabilities when, in the early hours of 15 April 1986, F-111Fs of the 48th

Tactical Fighter Wing, Lakenheath, struck at targets in Libya in a calculated response against growing international terrorism, allegedly supported by that nation. Although the operation was subsequently attended by much political controversy, the fact that the approval of the UK government for the launch of the F-111s and their supporting task force from British bases was sought and readily obtained was quite logical, in view of the 1951 Anglo-US agreement and its subsequent ratifications. Quite simply, the agreement makes provision for the offensive use of American air power from UK bases if such offensive use is deemed necessary in the interests of mutual security, and subject to joint decision. It is a matter of recorded history that both the US and UK governments had plenty of grounds for such action, and history yet to be written will probably record that they were right.

The build-up to the operation began in earnest on 11 April, when the US Third Air Force and USAFE were placed on alert to carry out an air strike on selected military targets in Libya. This was to be a concerted action with air elements of the United States Sixth Fleet, which was then on station between Sicily and the Gulf of Sirte. Within the next twelve hours the USAF's tanker task force in Britain was reinforced by the arrival of twenty-four McDonnell Douglas KC-10 Extenders, sixteen of which went to Mildenhall and the remainder to Fairford. Mildenhall's complement of fourteen KC-135 tankers was also increased to twenty aircraft, including a single KC-135Q; this variant, two of which were already located at Mildenhall, is used to refuel the SAC detachments of the 9th Strategic Reconnaissance Wing SR-71As.

The USAF's explanation for the tanker deployments was that they were in connection with a NATO exercise, 'Salty Nation', but as the weekend of 12–13 April progressed the level of USAF activity made it increasingly clear that a war operation was being prepared. At Lakenheath, the engines of a proportion of the 48th TFW's F-111Fs were being ground-run all through Saturday, and between 02.00 and 10.00 hours on Sunday eight more KC-10 tankers landed at Mildenhall, breaking the air base's long-standing ban on Sunday morning flying. The arrival of a large number of KC-10s was significant, because — unlike the KC-135 — they are equipped with both boom and probe-and-drogue refuelling systems, allowing them to refuel both US Navy and USAF aircraft. It was a sure indication that a combined operation was about to be mounted.

The operation itself was launched in the evening of Monday, 14 April, when elements of the tanker force departed from Mildenhall and Fairford to position themselves at intervals along the F-111s' approach route. The original plan had envisaged a flight of around 1,600 nautical miles directly across continental Europe but, since the French, Spanish and Italian governments had all refused permission for the strike force to overfly their territories, the route had to be rescheduled so that it crossed only international waters.

At 21.30 hours GMT on 14 April fifteen F-111Fs of the 48th TFW took off from RAF Lakenheath and were joined by three EF-111 Ravens from the 42nd Electronic Combat Squadron, RAF Upper Heyford. The total length of the flight, which now included a series of dog-legs to take it clear of France and Spain, was some 2,800 nautical miles, and as the F-111's combat radius with a 6,000-lb warload is about 1,000 nautical miles the outbound flight required three refuelling contacts. The first of these was made off the Cherbourg Peninsula, the F-111s subsequently continuing on a south-westerly heading out into the Atlantic before turning south to fly parallel with the Atlantic coasts of Spain and Portugal. The second refuelling contact was made west of Lisbon and the strike force then continued south before swinging east to pass through the Strait of Gibraltar. The flight so far had been made at high level, but the F-111s now descended to medium level for their third refuelling contact over the Mediterranean, off the Algerian coast.

With their tanks full again, the F-111 strike force now descended to low level, turning south at a point to the west of Sicily and by-passing the island of Lampedusa as they headed towards their assigned Libyan targets. There were three of these: the side of Tripoli Airport occupied by the Libyan Air Force, the Al Azziziyah barracks in Tripoli, and the Sidi Bilal port facility ten miles west of Tripoli, where the Libyan Navy based its Nanuchka-class missile corvettes and La Combattante missile patrol boats.

The F-111 formation split into three waves. Those aircraft tasked with the strike on the airfield and port facility were armed with Mk.20 Rockeye 500-lb laser-guided cluster bombs, while those assigned to the attack on the Tripoli barracks area and its associated command centre carried MK.82 laser-guided bombs for greater effect against hardened targets. At the same time, fifteen Grumman A-6 Intruders and Vought A-7 Corsairs from the Sixth Fleet carriers USS *America* and *Coral Sea*, also armed with 500-lb and 2,000-lb laser-guided weapons, headed in across the Gulf of Sirte to hit two targets near Benghazi: the Al Jumahiraya Barracks, which according to US Intelligence was a back-up command centre to the one at Tripoli, and the military airfield at Benina.

As the strike force made its final run towards the Libyan coast, top cover was provided by Sixth Fleet Grumman F-14 Tomcats and McDonnell Douglas F-18 Hornets as an insurance against possible activity by the Libyan Arab Air Force's MiG-23 and Mirage fighter force, but in the event there was none. The F-111s made single passes through the target areas at 550 knots, using their Pave Tack equipment; Libyan defences were effectively jammed by the EF-111 Ravens and also by US Navy Grumman EA-6 Prowlers. The attack was carried out through moderate and very inaccurate AAA and SAM fire. One F-111, piloted by Captain Fernando Ribas-Dominicci, from Puerto Rico, with Captain Paul Lorence from San Francisco as his weapons systems officer, was missing during the attack; its fate is unknown at the time of writing (1 May 1986). A second aircraft, thought to have gone missing also, in fact recovered safely to the US air base facility at Rota in Spain with engine trouble. All the remaining F-111s returned to the United Kingdom after flight refuelling en route.

Post-strike reconnaissance was carried out by two Lockheed SR-71A Blackbirds from Mildenhall, which photographed both target areas after dawn on 15 April from very high altitude. It revealed that all the assigned targets had been hit, albeit with a certain amount of collateral damage to civilians and civilian property in Tripoli, and a number of aircraft destroyed. These included MiG-23 fighters, Ilyushin Il-76 transports, Mi-8 transport helicopters and Mi-24 helicopter gunships.

Strangely enough, the presence of the potent F-111 in the United Kingdom had created very little fuss, at least by comparison with the later controversy surrounding the cruise missile, until the Libyan affair. The reason is probably psychological; the F-111 is there to be seen, whereas cruise missiles are kept under wraps, things of evil mystery and unknown potency. But 150 F-111s have the ability to inflict far more damage on a potential enemy in a wide variety of ways, and will retain it for some time to come. People are now aware of that fact, and from now on the 'Aardvark' is likely to be very much in the public eye.

8

The Unstable Seventies

IN THE EARLY 1970s a subtle — and, for NATO, worrying — series of changes were beginning to take effect on the military balance between East and West. A decade earlier the doctrine of massive retaliation had lost its credibility in the face of a major Soviet nuclear buildup; NATO had therefore adopted its strategy of flexible response, which was designed to provide not just strategic nuclear retaliation in the fact of aggression but a range of possible reactions proportional to the challenge, including conventional defence, a range of theatre nuclear responses, and a general strategic nuclear option. Conventional forces, theatre forces, and strategic nuclear forces now constituted the triad on which NATO depended for deterrence: it was, however, a vulnerable triad.

The thinking behind flexible response was that a potential aggressor, unable to forecast the nature of NATO's response to an attack but certain that NATO had great flexibility in deciding how to respond or to escalate as necessary, would be deterred by the high risk associated with adventurism. It failed, however, to take into account the somewhat different approach of the Soviet Union's military planners.

As the 1970s progressed it became clear to the Russians that NATO might not use nuclear weapons from the outset of war, and that indeed NATO chiefs might be reluctant to authorise nuclear release at all because of the horrific consequences. The many peace movements advocating unilateral disarmament and the widespread publicity in the West accorded to the horrors of nuclear war, together with accompanying political arguments, all served in Soviet eyes to increase the pressure on

NATO leaders to interpret flexible response as implying that NATO would initially only defend itself by means of conventional weapons, and would use nuclear weapons only as a last desperate measure to avoid total defeat.

During the era of US strategic superiority the size and character of Soviet long-range theatre nuclear forces were of less importance to NATO than they have been since the early 1970s, as the Russians could have expected any action taken with those forces in Europe to evoke a response from superior US intercontinental forces. With the emergence of parity in central strategic systems, however, the Russians came to believe — however incorrectly — that they could use or threaten to use their long-range theatre nuclear forces in the expectation that the US would be deterred from responding with its central strategic systems.

Parity in central strategic systems therefore increased the importance of NATO's long-range theatre nuclear forces because the lack of a credible military response at this level created a serious gap in NATO's continuum of deterrence and defence. Before 1977, when the 48th Tactical Fighter Wing received its complement of F-111s at Lakenheath, NATO's long-range theatre nuclear force consisted of the 20th TFWs seventy-two F-111s at Upper Heyford and fifty-odd Vulcan B.2 bombers of No. 1 Group, RAF Strike Command, distributed among six squadrons at RAF Scampton and RAF Waddington.

Although long in the tooth, the Vulcan was still a viable weapons system, and was to remain so until the late 1970s when detachments of four aircraft from Waddington went to the United States to take part in Red Flag, the air warfare exercise held under realistic conditions in the Arizona Desert. The Vulcans operated at night, and despite the fact that the ground was not ideal for terrain following some good results were achieved, showing that the Vulcan still had the ability to penetrate sophisticated defence systems. And whatever the Vulcan could do, apart from carry a massive bomb load, the F-111 could do better. Nevertheless, NATO's long-range tactical nuclear force remained static throughout the 1970s, and as Soviet defences improved its offensive capability — particularly that of the aging Vulcan — became increasingly compromised.

The vulnerability of aircraft engaged in deep-penetration raids into heavily defended enemy territory, already exposed in the Vietnam War, was demonstrated again in the Middle East War of October 1972, when Egypt and Syria attacked Israel on two fronts. The two surprising developments in the first few days of the war were the effectiveness of the Arab air defences and the deadly accuracy of Soviet-supplied anti-tank weapons. The air defence was based on a combination of the mobile SA-6 surface-to-air missile and the four-barrel ZSU-23/4 Shilka radar-controlled mobile anti-aircraft gun system.

During the first three days of the war, which began on 6 October, the Israeli air and armoured forces suffered fearful losses; then the Syrians and Egyptians began to exhaust their supplies of missiles, enabling the Israelis to launch effective counterattacks. Almost immediately the Russians, apparently honouring a commitment made before the war, began to resupply their clients; the first shipload of supplies left Odessa on 7 October, by 10 October an airlift of equipment to Syria and Egypt was under way, and by 12 October they were making between 60 and 90 flights a day. On that same day, President Richard Nixon ordered an immediate airlift to aid Israel. Skyhawks and Phantoms to replace aircraft lost by the Israeli Air Force were flown direct to Israel, while new tanks, self-propelled guns, helicopters, anti-tank missiles, ammunition and spare parts were also airlifted for the sake of speed. Between mid-October and mid-November Lockheed C-5 Galaxys and C-141 Starlifters delivered 22,400 tons of cargo in 566 separate flights.

By 16 October the Israelis had contained the Syrians and were able to concentrate on the Suez front. Pushing an armoured force across the Suez Canal, they began to roll up Egyptian SAM sites, making it possible for Israeli fighter-bombers to operate effectively in support of the ground forces, and the Egyptian 3rd Army found itself surrounded. On 24 October Egypt's President Sadat asked President Nixon and Russia's President Brezhnev to send a joint American-Soviet force to enforce a UN ceasefire; Brezhnev informed Nixon that if the US would not move in with them, the Russians would go it alone.

The American response was a Defense Condition Three alert for all US forces worldwide, a drastic response based on intelligence reports that the Russians were about to fly several battalions of airborne troops to Egypt and the knowledge that the Soviet Naval Squadron in the Mediterranean had been increased from 60 to 84 ships, outnumbering the US Sixth Fleet.

DefCon Three — which placed US forces on a high state of readiness, if not actually on a war footing — came as something of a surprise to Third Air Force personnel in Britain. Married servicemen stationed around the various US bases were sent home for their battle kit — CBW warfare clothing and so on — and told to return immediately. From Mildenhall, HQ of the Third Air Force since the closure of South Ruislip in 1972, Hercules transport of the 513th Tactical Airlift Wing ran a steady shuttle service carrying spares and other equipment to the fighter-bomber bases. The net result of the US alert was a Soviet signal that no troops would be sent to the Middle East, and the Americans put pressure on the Israelis to cease offensive operations against the Egyptian 3rd Army.

At the time of the Middle East alert, the Order of Battle of the US Third Air Force was as follows. The 10th Tactical Reconnaissance Wing was still at RAF Alconbury with RF-4C Phantoms; in 1965 it had lost control of the 19th and 42nd Tactical Reconnaissance Squadrons with the formation of the 26th TRW under 17th Air Force command, and it now comprised the 1st, 30th and 32nd TRS. RAF Bentwaters housed the 91st and 92nd Squadrons of the 81st Tactical Fighter Wing, with F-4D Phantoms: the 78th TFS was at Woodbridge, which was also the home of the HC-130 Hercules and HH-3E helicopters of the 67th Aerospace Rescue and Recovery Squadron. Greenham Common remained a standby base operated by the 7551st Combat Support Group and was used from time to time by transport aircraft engaged in Reforger reinforcement exercises; in 1976 it was the temporary home for three months of the 20th TFW's F-111s, which moved there while the runways at Upper Heyford were being resurfaced.

The 48th TFW, with F-4D Phantoms, at Lakenheath was eagerly awaiting conversion to new equipment, although it would be 1977 before the Wing began to receive F-111s. RAF Mildenhall, Third Air Force Headquarters, housed the C-130s of the 513th Tactical Airlift Wing, the EC-135s of the Airborne Command Post, the 435th Tactical Airlift Wing (a headquarters unit of Military Air Command responsible for handling C-130 wings on bi-monthly detachment from the United States), and Detachment One of the 306th Strategic Wing, which operated the KC-135s of the European Tanker Task Force. The potent F-111s of the 20th Tactical Fighter Wing were at Upper Heyford, exercising their primary role of NATO theatre strike force.

At Alconbury, the 32nd and 30th TRS were deactivated on 1 January and 1 April 1976 respectively, and their RF-4Cs were assigned to Air National Guard units in the United States. This was part of a reshuffle designed to make room for the formation at Alconbury on 1 April 1976 of a new and unique unit in USAFE: the 527th Tactical Fighter Training Aggressor Squadron. The Squadron's task was — and still is — to provide combat tactics training for USAF units in Europe, and for this purpose it was equipped with the Northrop F-5E Tiger II, a highly manoeuvrable day/night fighter with a limited all-weather capability.

The first eight of the Squadron's twenty F-5Es arrived at Alconbury on 21 May 1976 aboard a giant C-5A Galaxy transport from the Air Logistics Center at McClellan AFB, California, the aircraft packed in specially designed pallets with the wings and various other parts removed from the fuselage. After reassembly, engine testing and inspection, the first flight took place on 1 June 1976. Two more Galaxy flights arrived during June with the remainder of the Squadron's aircraft, enabling the 527th to test and validate its training concepts and procedures before being declared fully operational on 1 January 1977.

First flown in August 1972, the F-5E Tiger II is an advanced version of the Northrop F-5 Freedom Fighter, which was widely exported to NATO air forces. Powered by two General Electric J85 turbojets, each producing 5,000 pounds of thrust with afterburning, the F-5E can fly at 1,000 mph and reach an altitude of 50,000 feet. Built-in armament is two 20-mm cannon

Close-up of the A-10's GAU-8/A 30-mm seven-barrel rotary cannon, which can fire 4,200 rounds per minute of armour-piercing ammunition.

A Boeing KC-135 Stratotanker of the European Tanker Task Force, RAF Mildenhall.

A Lockheed C-141B Starlifter of the 437th Military Airlift Wing on the approach to land at Mildenhall. The Starlifter can carry forty tons of freight at a speed of 460 mph.

A Lockheed C-5A Galaxy at Greenham Common. Mightiest of the Military Air Command's transports, it was the Galaxy that brought much of the original cruise missile equipment to the UK.

Lockheed HC-130H Hercules of the 67th Aerospace Rescue and Recovery Squadron, Woodbridge. This version of the Hercules was developed for survivor and astronaut recovery and features a retractable nose yoke which can snatch a survivor to safety by means of a nylon life-line attached to a balloon.

Lockheed HC-130P Hercules fuels a Sikorsky HH-3E 'Jolly Green Giant' rescue helicopter in mid-air. Both aircraft belong to the 67th ARRS, Woodbridge. The bulge on the Hercules' fuselage, forward of the wing, houses satellite re-entry tracking equipment to aid recovery of reconnaissance capsules.

The sinister-looking Lockheed SR-71 Blackbird long-range reconnaissance aircraft. The UK base used by this type is Mildenhall, from where its missions are conducted with the utmost secrecy. The SR-71 can fly at three times the speed of sound at heights of up to 100,000 feet.

Latest addition to the European Tanker Task Force is the KC-10A Extender, a military version of the McDonnell Douglas DC-10 airliner. This one is pictured at Mildenhall's annual air fete.

in the nose, with 280 rounds per gun, and the aircraft can carry two AIM-9 Sidewinder air-to-air missiles on wingtip launchers and up to 7,000 pounds of mixed ordnance under the wings and fuselage.

Before the 527th Squadron was activated, the F-5E had already proved its value with the 4440th Aggressor Squadron at Nellis Air Force Base in Nevada, where realistic Red Flag exercises are held under simulated war conditions. With a wingspan of only twenty-six feet and a length of just over forty-eight feet, the Tiger II was similar in both size and radar signature to the MiG-21, in the early 1970s the most common Warsaw Pact tactical aircraft, and to make things even more realistic the Aggressor F-5s were painted in Warsaw Pact camouflage patterns. Their pilots specialised in Soviet fighter tactics, which was essential if the air combat training they provided was to have any real value.

The reason behind the formation of the Aggressor squadrons was that, at the beginning of the 1970s, the Soviet Frontovaya Aviatsiya (Tactical Air Force) was equipping with highly sophisticated aircraft which, across the board, were more manoeuvrable than most NATO types then in service. So, in providing what was known as DACT (Dissimilar Air Combat Tactics) training the members of the 527th Aggressor Squadron and their counterparts at Nellis AFB stressed the important areas of combat training and air-to-air exercises, as well as providing academic instruction on all aspects of the Soviet/Warsaw Pact air defence system.

Training of USAFE and NATO fighter crews by the 527th Squadron, which was assigned to the 10th Tactical Reconnaissance Wing, was organised into three stages. In the first, the pilots undergoing DACT flew against the Tigers in basic size and performance exercises, one-versus-one sorties designed to expose the fighter crews to the advantages and disadvantages of pitting themselves against Soviet-type aircraft, which were generally smaller and had lower wing loadings than comparable western types.

The second stage consisted of offensive and defensive exercises involving multiple aircraft, usually on a two-versus-one basis, with the emphasis on teamwork, radio procedures and flight discipline and with the basis of fluid tactics being reviewed throughout. Disengagement tactics were frequently practised during this phase because they laid stress on the team effort necessary for the fighter pilots to get in, complete their mission and get out as a unit. In counteroffensive exercises the fighter crews were initially placed in various positions of disadvantage from which they had to extricate themselves by reacting quickly to a given situation. The objective was to react to a defensive situation as a fighting unit and either turn the dogfight to an offensive position or disengage, depending on the tactical situation.

The third and last stage of the course involved greater numbers of aircraft — for example, two-versus-two and two-versus-four — in which the fighter crews made use of the lessons learned on previous missions to practise more dynamic and tactically flexible scenarios such as they would be likely to encounter in an actual war situation.

Initially, the activities of the 527th Squadron over the Wash, the East Anglian coast and the North Sea caused more than a little confusion when the crews of civil aircraft operating in the area flew through the middle of the mock-combat zones without being aware of their existence. In 1976, while the Aggressors were working up to operational standard, Fokker Friendship airliners of Air Anglia, flying on the 'oil rig route' from Norwich to Aberdeen with about thirty passengers, were involved in three airmiss incidents.

On one occasion an F-5E appeared from underneath a Friendship and climbed straight in front of it at a range of less than half a mile. The 527th's commander, Colonel MacLennan, admitted: 'We didn't know it and they didn't know it. They were just going straight through from 12,000 to about 15,000 feet. Our radar control told us to knock it off because there was a stranger in the area. At present there is no official system for contacting the civilian side; NATO didn't feel it necessary because it is an established military training area.'

The incidents produced better liaison between the civil and military authorities in that area, and everything was sorted out satisfactorily, but civil pilots still keep an extra-sharp lookout in case they are suddenly confronted by something that looks like a Russian jet fighter.

In April 1977 HQ Third Air Force entered into preliminary but as yet informal discussions with the UK Ministry of Defence on the possibility of reactivating Greenham Common as a base for some twenty KC-135 tanker aircraft following a planned expansion of the European Tanker Task Force: Mildenhall was already overcrowded and Greenham had a great deal more to offer in the way of facilities than other standby bases such as Sculthorpe. No formal agreement was reached at that time, but in August work began on refurbishing and extending Greenham's runways and it was clear to the local population that something was afoot. When a formal request to reopen Greenham as a tanker base was made in February 1978, the news brought a storm of protest from the residents of Newbury and the surrounding area.

In the space of four weeks the hurriedly organised Campaign Against the Reactivation of Greenham Common Air Base staged a silent protest march through Newbury, collected 16,000 signatures, and had a prolonged audience with Mr Fred Mulley, the Secretary of State for Defence. The protesters pointed out that the community around Greenham had expanded greatly since the SAC mission ended in 1964, and that there was now a greater concentration of houses, schools and hospitals within two miles of the end of the runway than at any other airfield in Britain; their estimates indicated that about 10,000 residents would suffer intolerable noise levels, and 40,000 more severe disturbance. There were also twelve schools, with 6,000 pupils, within two miles of the western end of the runway: according to the headmaster of one local school, Mr Ray Pedley, O Level GCE passes had fallen by nearly fifty per cent in 1976, and he believed that the noise created by the F-111s on temporary deployment from Upper Heyford had been at least partly to blame.

Mr Pedley's belief was not without foundation: the sortie rate of the F-111s had been high and there was no doubt that the noise they made had created severe disturbance. What, then, would it be like if the KC-135s arrived, for the jet tanker was reputedly one of the noisiest aircraft in the USAF?

There was no doubt that the KC-135 was a very noisy aircraft indeed — the Pentagon had admitted as much some months earlier in a statement that was now to give fuel to the protesters' case and cause much embarrassment in US official circles. Unlike the civilian Boeing 707 airliner from which it was developed, the KC-135 had no noise baffles on its engines, and with 26,000 gallons of fuel on board it required a lengthy take-off run followed by a shallow climb-out, which meant that its noise pattern was spread over a wide area. According to the protesters, who had done some thorough homework, the area in the immediate vicinity of the airfield would be subject to around 112 PNdB (perceived noise decibels) which was acknowledged to be close to the threshold of pain; the noise level within about six miles of a KC-135 starting its take-off roll would be twice that permitted at night (102PNdB) four miles from that point at London Heathrow; and by day the Greenham levels would be forty per cent greater than those permitted at Heathrow (108 PNdb).

Not all the residents of the Newbury area were opposed to the KC-135s coming to Greenham; at the Kennet School, sixth formers set about collecting signatures in support of the idea. But the anti-tanker campaigners had by far the greater degree of support, and their protest gathered momentum with deputations to the US Embassy and plans to send a female delegation to deliver a personal protest to President Jimmy Carter. In the end the protesters carried the day; on 26 May 1978 Mr James Wellbeloved, the Under-Secretary of State for the RAF, announced that the proposal to base the tankers at Greenham Common had been rejected.

Mr Wellbeloved said that Mr Fred Mulley, the Secretary for Defence, had decided against the scheme because of the possible hazards from the aircraft flying over the Atomic Energy Establishment at Aldermaston. However, he told the House that the government had agreed in principle that the additional tankers would be based in this country and a decision on their new location would be taken within the next few days at a meeting at the Ministry of Defence. Referring to Aldermaston, Mr Wellbeloved said: 'Although aircraft approaching Greenham Common would not normally overfly the prohibited airspace which surrounds this establishment for safety reasons, one cannot rule out the possibility that one of these aircraft might inadvertently infringe this airspace. While we would not rule out the use of Greenham Common by more manoeuvrable aircraft, it does seem an unnecessary risk to take in peacetime when there are alternative locations.'

On the face of it, Aldermaston seems to have been used as a rather lame excuse to cover up the real fact that the government had been forced to back down in the face of overwhelming public opinion. Among the protesters there was jubilation. 'Isn't it wonderful news?' cried one of them, Mrs Lynette Edwell. 'We have won a great victory, but the battle is not yet over. While it has been made clear that we will not be getting the KC-135s, it hasn't been made clear that Greenham airfield will not be reactivated. We will continue our fight until that assurance has been given.' And in the words of another, Mrs Lorraine Leigh: 'The decision has lifted a heavy cloud from over Newbury. The last fourteen weeks of protest and hard work have really been worthwhile.'

They were, of course, unaware that an even greater storm of protest was soon to burst over Greenham Common; in the light of events that were soon to unfold, the people of Newbury might have done well to accept the tankers, with all their associated noise. But in the summer of 1958 few people outside US military circles had heard of cruise missiles.

There remained the thorny problem of where the KC-135s were to be based. The two most likely locations were Fairford, which had been vacated by RAF Air Support Command in 1971 and so appeared the obvious choice, and Brize Norton, which housed the VC-10 long-range jet transports of No. 10 Squadron RAF and was still active. Protest movements developed at both locations and particularly at Fairford, which had a taste of the KC-135 in September 1978 when six aircraft were deployed there to take part in the annual series of NATO exercises code-named Autumn Forge. The news that the MoD had agreed to the use of Fairford by the Strategic Air Command tankers had broken a few weeks earlier, so the arrival of the first two KC-135s on 7 September came as no real surprise.

These two aircraft carried out a series of noise tests over the following week and evoked mixed reactions from the local community. 'Horrendous', said Don Russett, an accountant who lived barely a mile from the runway and who headed the local action committee. 'It was unbearable in villages under the flight path. Any permanency of these planes being stationed at Fairford has to be stopped.'

An opposite opinion was volunteered by another local, tractor-driver Michael Bolton. 'Just kid's play,' he said. 'It was noisy, but it isn't going to cause trouble to the cattle. Concorde [tested at Fairford in the early 1970s] didn't either. If the cattle are born on the farm, they just get used to it.'

The protesters had the wind knocked out of their sails when, later in the month at the close of the noise trials, the Cotswold District Council's planning and development committee announced that it accepted that Fairford was the 'only suitable base in the short term.' The Cotswold District Council itself rejected the plan only two days later, but it made no difference; the presence of the KC-135s at Fairford was a fait accompli, and from then on the base was to see regular visits by Stratotankers from the 34th Strategic Squadron at Zaragoza, Spain, and the 922nd Strategic Squadron at Hellenikon in Greece, both forming part of the Strategic Air Command's 11th Strategic Group.

While the tanker controversy was in full swing the Third Air Force and, to a lesser extent, the Ministry of Defence found themselves with another major confrontation — this time against the Trade Unions. It all started in July 1978, when British steelworkers helping to build hardened aircraft shelters at Lakenheath, Alconbury, Bentwaters and Woodbridge went on strike over a pay dispute. An Italian company, Cimolai, had been contracted by NATO to erect the steel reinforcing in the shelters and they in turn had sub-contracted the hiring of labour to a British firm, Carter Horsley. A protest strike led to the sacking of fifty workers and pickets were set up at the four air bases, seriously affecting the site work. In August, with the number on strike having risen to 80, Italian labour was brought in to complete the work, and this move provoked a bitter reaction from the Trade Union movement.

Mr Ken Weech, Labour MP for the Ipswich constituency

that included Woodbridge, demanded an immediate government enquiry into the dispute. 'It is unprecedented in this
country to bring in foreign blackleg labour to break a strike,' he
declared. 'I have been in touch with all parties concerned to try
and sort out who allowed these Italians to come in, but have
come up against a wall of silence, which I regard as sinister.'
Mr Weech said he had received a letter from the Department of
Environment, which advised that under EEC regulations there
could be no objections to Italians working in Britain. Indeed,
the letter stated, there could be a good deal of embarrassment if
their employment were resisted.

Nevertheless, resisted it was, and on 2 September police had
to be called to Woodbridge after pickets threatened to overturn
a van carrying eight Italians. For some weeks the situation was
very tense, particularly as several hundred workers belonging
to other unions had been laid off because of the dispute, and
support for the strikers gradually swelled. At last, early in
October, the Italian construction workers were withdrawn, as
were the pickets at the four air bases concerned; a new pay deal
was negotiated, the sacked workers were reinstated and work
on the aircraft shelters was resumed after a delay of three
months.

The strike had one immediate consequence: early in December it was announced that a 400-strong squad of USAF airfield
construction engineers of the Rapid Emergency Deployable
Heavy Operation Repair Squadron Engineering ('Red Horse')
would be based at Wethersfield from April 1979. Their osten-
sible function would be runway repair, but they could carry out
other engineering tasks as well — including building work
normally undertaken by civilian contractors.

The provision of hardened shelters and other facilities was
particularly vital at Bentwaters and Woodbridge, for the 81st
Tactical Fighter Wing was in the throes of expansion and
conversion and would soon become the biggest wing in the
United States Air Force. In the closing months of 1978, pilots
from the Bentwaters-based 92nd Tactical Fighter Squadron
had gone to Davis-Monthan AFB in Arizona to begin conversion to a radical new combat aircraft, the Fairchild A-10
Thunderbolt II.

The A-10 concept arose during the Vietnam War, which exposed the serious lack of an aircraft designed specifically for ground attack and close support. This lack was particularly acute in the European context, where any future conflict would begin with massive conventional air strikes and armoured thrusts by the Warsaw Pact forces, rather than with the nuclear attack that had once been envisaged. What NATO needed, and badly, was an aircraft that could kill enemy tanks in all weathers and survive in an environment dominated by enemy SAMs, fighters and the deadly Shilka anti-aircraft artillery.

The aircraft that emerged to fulfil this task, the A-10 Thunderbolt, was quite remarkably ugly, a fact reflected in its unofficial name, Warthog. It is very heavily armoured, the pilot sitting in a titanium 'bathtub', and the airframe has a built-in redundant structure policy, which means that the pilot can retain control even if large portions of the airframe are shot away. The A-10's built-in firepower is its massive GAU-8/A 30-mm seven-barrel rotary cannon, which is mounted on the centreline under the forward fuselage. The gun fires up to 4,200 rounds per minute of armour-piercing ammunition with cores of depleted (non-radioactive) uranium for greater impact, and is quite capable of destroying a light tank or armoured fighting vehicle. The aircraft also has eight underwing and three under-fuselage attachments for up to 16,000 pounds of bombs, missiles, gun pods and jammer pods, and carries the Pave Penny laser system pod for target designation, while avionics include a central air data computer, an inertial navigation system and a head-up display.

For the former Phantom pilots of the 92nd TFS, the transition to the A-10 began with five conversion flights and a number of attack sorties using all the aircraft's combinations of weaponry, followed by more weapons-training flights under realistic tactical conditions, and then twelve sorties designed to familiarise them with the tactics employed by USAFE in battlefront situations.

The operation to replace the 81st TFW's Phantoms with A-10s was code-named Ready Thunder. By way of a preliminary, four A-10s of the 57th Fighter Weapons Wing at Nellis AFB, Nevada, visited Bentwaters on 21 February 1978; all were on their way back to the US after being involved in Maverick anti-tank missile trials in Germany. The 81st TFW began to receive its own A-10s in January 1979, and over the next seven months the type equipped the 78th, 91st, and 510th Tactical Fighter Squadrons as well as the 92nd. The last squadron, together with the 510th, moved up to Sembach for operational training while the 78th went to Ahlhorn; the 91st stayed at Bentwaters, where it was joined in 1980 by the 509th and 511th TFS, bringing total strength of the 81st TFW to six squadrons and 108 aircraft.

From its main bases at Bentwaters and Woodbridge the 81st TFW continues to deploy its squadrons to Forward Operating Locations in West Germany. Of necessity, A-10 pilots must be more familiar with the West German terrain than anyone except, perhaps, helicopter crews and the pilots of the RAF's V/STOL Harrier force. The Warthogs usually deploy to their FOLs in clutches of eight or nine; each FOL has a computer link with Bentwaters, so that when spares are needed they can be rapidly flown out, as can ground crews to undertake major servicing. This arrangement does away with the need to maintain large stocks of spares and additional personnel in Germany, thereby easing logistics problems.

Because the A-10 is designed to fly a very high sortie rate, servicing is made as simple as possible to cut down turnround time. Most of the aircraft's inspection panels can be reached by a man standing on the ground, and an automatic system facilitates rapid reloading of the 1,350-round GAU-8/A ammunition drum. The fact that the 81st TFW has been known to fly eighty-six sorties with eleven aircraft in one day gives a good idea of the aircraft's capability; in fact, the limiting factor on sortie rate is pilot fatigue — which is high in the A-10, for operational sorties require a great deal of high-g manoeuvring at low level.

The A-10s operate in two-ship flights, each covering a swathe of ground up to six miles wide. In practice, the best swathe width has been found to be two or three miles, so that an attack can quickly be mounted by the second aircraft once the first pilot has made his firing pass on the target. The A-10 has a combat radius of 250 nautical miles, enough to reach a target area on the East German border from a FOL in central

Germany and then move on to another target area in northern Germany. The aircraft has a three and a half hour loiter endurance, though wartime sorties in Europe would probably last between one and two hours, and the 30-mm ammunition drum carries enough rounds to make up to 15 firing passes.

The Warthog pilots of the 81st TFW maintain that in time of war their main worry would be the proximity of the ground, rather than enemy AAA or fighters: the A-10 is a big aircraft, and in a vertical bank the wingtip is twenty-five feet closer to the ground than the pilot, so pilots learn to do flat turns, especially when manoeuvring under low cloud. Its best turning performance gives the Warthog a turning circle of only 4,000 feet diameter, and the aircraft is fitted with an audible stall warning device so that the pilot can concentrate on the task in hand rather than worry about his speed falling away to a dangerous level.

The A-10 can operate from short, unprepared strips less than 1,500 feet long; there are literally thousands of fields that fall into this category in West Germany, as well as sections of road to which the aircraft can be deployed from their FOLs. Once in the combat area, the A-10 pilot can engage enemy armour at a range of between 4,000 and 6,000 feet; in fact, his gunsight is calibrated at the 4,000-foot range mark. This, coupled with the aircraft's turning circle of 4,000 feet, means that the pilot can engage a target without having to pass over it. A one-second burst will place seventy rounds of 30-mm shells on the target, and as a complete 360-degree turn takes no more than sixteen seconds two A-10s can bring continuous fire to bear.

To survive in a hostile environment dominated by his principal enemy, the ZSU-23/4 Shilka, the Warthog pilot must fly at 100 feet or less and never remain straight and level for more than four seconds. Survivability also depends on close co-operation between the two A-10s; while one engages the target, the other stands off and engages anti-aircraft installations with its TV-guided Maverick missiles, up to six of which can be carried. If the Warthog is attacked by an enemy fighter, the standard tactic is to turn head-on towards the attacker and spray him with 30-mm ammunition.

All things considered, the A-10 is one of the most formid-able weapons in NATO's battlefield arsenal. It could create havoc with a Soviet armoured thrust, a fact that undoubtedly places its rear bases of Bentwaters and Woodbridge very high on the target list for Russia's SS-20 medium-range missiles.

9

The Cruise Missile Controversy

BY THE MID-1970s NATO Intelligence had become aware that the Soviet Union was developing a new intermediate-range ballistic missile, which was given the NATO designation SS-X-20 — simplified to SS-20 once it had reached operational status — to replace the weapons then deployed against Western Europe

The new missile appeared to have an interesting development history. In 1965 the Soviet Union had publicly displayed what seemed to be its first solid-fuel ICBM, the SS-13, designed to be housed in underground silos and supposedly the equivalent of America's Minuteman. It entered service in 1968, but only about sixty were deployed before manufacture terminated in 1970: the Russians, it seemed, were concentrating on the development of a mobile version known to the West as the SS-16.

However, during SS-16 flight tests, which were closely observed by the United States, the first of the missile's three stages consistently failed to meet the specified performance, possibly because the Soviet chemical industry did not have the technology to produce solid-fuel rocket motors of the size and thrust required for the first stage of an ICBM. On the other hand, the second and third stages worked perfectly well and provided a ready-made basis for the development of a new IRBM. The result was the SS-20, deployment of which began in 1977.

Almost overnight the SS-20 upset the whole East-West strategic balance — a balance that was already very fine, with the Soviet Strategic Rocket Forces having started to deploy extremely accurate ICBMs which were cold-launched from their silos by gas pressure before the rocket motors were ignited, allowing the silos to be reloaded.

The first of the new-generation ICBMs was the SS-18 (Soviet designation RS-20), the largest ICBM in the world, which was first deployed in 1974. Its silos, which were later modified for the cold-launch technique, are specially hardened to withstand pressures of up to 6,000 pounds per square inch, making them virtually invulnerable to anything less than a direct hit by a thermonuclear warhead. The two-stage SS-18 can carry an immensely powerful warhead — or combination of warheads — over a range of 7,500 miles, and most of the 308 currently deployed are thought to be fitted with ten 500-kiloton MIRVs targeted on the US Minuteman missile fields.

Because of the ability of its silos to withstand a missile attack, the SS-18 practically demolished the West's deterrent credibility in the mid-1970s. Moreover, its deployment was followed by that of two more highly accurate ICBMs, the SS-17 (RS-16) and SS-19 (RS-18), both of which can carry up to six 500-kiloton MIRVs over a range of 6,200 miles. About sixty of the total 300 SS-19s in service are reported to be assigned to targets in Western Europe.

Formidable though these weapons are, they are all fixed-site weapons subject to constant satellite surveillance, their locations known and targeted by Strategic Air Command. With the deployment of the SS-20, however, the Soviet Union was provided with a missile system whose mobility made it virtually impossible to detect. Moreover, the missile's estimated range of 4,600 miles with a single 50-kt MIRV (or 2,500 miles with three 150-kt MIRVs) meant that it threatened all the European NATO nations from bases inside Soviet territory.

NATO had nothing to compare with the SS-20. The only counter to it within the European Theatre was the UK-based strike force of F-111s at Upper Heyford and Lakenheath, and the deployment of the SS-20 made their bases highly vulnerable. What was needed to counter the new threat was another mobile missile system, easy to disperse and carrying a nuclear warhead, which would release aircraft such as the F-111 from the need to be held nuclear-ready to counter a

Soviet in-theatre missile attack and free them for conventional operations.

The underlying need was to restore credibility to NATO's policy of flexible response, which required a full complement of effective weapons at four distinct levels: conventional, battle-field nuclear, theatre nuclear and strategic warfare. If the level of response at any of the first three stages became seriously weakened, a Soviet attack on Europe would almost certainly lead to a global nuclear exchange. Another factor was the growing ability of the Soviet Union to destroy NATO air bases, particularly those in the United Kingdom, using Backfire and Fencer bombers armed with long-range stand-off weapons, which would leave NATO devoid of a theatre nuclear response.

The choice, then, was stark. If NATO's theatre nuclear forces were knocked out at an early stage in any future conflict, the Alliance would either have to rely on its conventional forces to stem a Soviet assault — with an almost inevitable escalation to battlefield nuclear weapons, given the Soviet Union's vast conventional superiority — or resort to submarine-launched ballistic missiles. In either event a swift move up the ladder of escalation would be the likely outcome. By the beginning of 1979, with the deployment of SS-20 well under way, the situation was regarded as becoming dangerously unstable.

The result was that a special meeting of NATO foreign and defence ministers on 12 December 1979 decided to embark on a programme of long-range theatre nuclear force modernisation. Briefly, the decision involved the replacement of existing Pershing 1A tactical missiles deployed in the Federal Republic of Germany with 108 longer-range Pershing IIs, and the deployment of 464 ground-launched cruise missiles (GLCMs) on the territory of a number of the European Allies. Germany, Britain, Italy, the Netherlands and Belgium agreed in principle to host these weapons, though the Dutch and Belgians delayed their final acceptance. While some of the costs of the deployments would be borne by NATO's infrastructure programme, all the new missiles would be American-owned; however, as with all other US nuclear weapons deployed in Europe, they would be subject to well understood NATO constraints and guidelines. Each of the new missiles was to have a single warhead, and as well as replacing 572 existing warheads they would enable a further 1,000 theatre nuclear warheads to be withdrawn from Europe.

The decision to introduce new long-range weapons into NATO's nuclear arsenal was only one element, albeit a controversial one, in a pattern of theatre nuclear modernisation that had been going on for many years. From the very beginning of its existence the theatre nuclear stockpile available to NATO had been subject to change, with old systems withdrawn as new ones were introduced, and while its overall size had remained relatively static since the late 1960s, there had been significant changes in its character and composition. In the first place, greater attention had been given to the physical security of the weapons and to insuring against their seizure or unauthorised use; at the same time, new weapons had emphasised greater accuracy coupled with lower yield warheads in order to reduce the risk of undesirable collateral damage.

The decision to modernise the long-range theatre nuclear force, however, represented a major change of emphasis: the withdrawal of 1,000 nuclear warheads would ultimately result in a substantial reduction in the overall size of the stockpile, but the introduction of the new missiles would shift its balance towards longer range systems. The really significant consequence of the new deployments was that they increased the ability of the Alliance to deliver warheads on Soviet territory from bases in Western Europe. This in turn thrust the whole issue of what have been termed by the Soviet Union 'forward based systems' into renewed prominence.

Another factor in the proposed deployment of modernised LRTNF — although this did not really emerge until after the NATO decision to deploy the weapons had been taken — was a revision of the American strategic posture. The new US 'countervailing strategy' stemmed from a major review of targeting policy and of the requirements for continued credible deterrence, and instructions for its implementation were issued on 25 September 1980 in the form of Presidential Directive 59.

Basically, the object was to increase the flexibility of American strategic forces by increasing the range of targeting options available in the hope of reinforcing deterrence against less than all-out attacks on either the United States or its allies, and thereby reinforcing the credibility of extended deterrence. American spokesmen stressed that the countervailing strategy was not new, but that it had evolved from established strategic concepts and policies. However, it did reflect a recognition on the part of the American policy-makers that a posture of assured destruction alone was an inadequate basis for the American strategic commitment to Europe. What the revised posture sought to do, in effect, was to reinforce the link between strategic and theatre nuclear forces by providing for more flexible options at the strategic level. Within such a strategic posture, the function of modernised long-range theatre nuclear forces was to close the gap between strategic weapons and the shorter-range tactical systems.

Before examining the deployment of cruise missiles in Britain, and the consequent involvement of the US Third Air Force, it is useful at this point to take a look at the nuclear capability of Britain herself, because much of it depended on weapons that came under Third Air Force control. In 1980 Britain had possessed her own nuclear weapons for nearly thirty years, and it had been the policy of successive governments to align the UK nuclear forces ever more closely with NATO. All British nuclear forces therefore were (and are) without exception assigned to the Alliance and included in the plans of the Supreme Allied Commander Europe (SACEUR) and the Supreme Allied Commander Atlantic (SACLANT).

In comparison with those of the United States, Britain's nuclear forces were small, although in certain areas they were numerically important. For example, Britain provided a significant proportion of the longer range aircraft available to SACEUR for nuclear missions, and the bulk of the theatre nuclear forces in the Eastern Atlantic. Their value, however, lay not so much in their numerical addition to NATO's strength, but rather in the fact that while fully NATO-committed they came under separate control, giving the Russians two nuclear powers to worry about, inevitably complicating both their judgement and their planning and increasing the risks and uncertainties they would face as a consequence of any aggression against NATO. This explains why the Soviet Union always insisted on the UK deterrent forces being weighed in the balance during strategic arms limitation talks.

When the Conservative Party took power in May 1979 they inherited a nuclear deterrent comprising four nuclear-powered submarines, each carrying sixteen Polaris missiles. Already under way was a £1,000-million programme to give Polaris a new payload, with decoys and other penetration aids which would ensure that the six warheads fitted to each missile reached their targets despite improvements in Soviet ballistic missile defences. This system, called Chevaline, was designed, managed and paid for by the United Kingdom, with the full cooperation of the United States, and consists of six 40-kiloton warheads; the payload can be manoeuvred in space, with a maximum spacing of 40 miles between individual warhead impact points, and is designed to keep Polaris viable until the planned Trident fleet becomes operational in the early 1990s.

In addition to the Polaris missile force, the United Kingdom also made a contribution to NATO's short-range theatre nuclear forces, deploying a number of systems equipped with American nuclear weapons and operated on a dual key basis. These included a regiment of Lance surface-to-surface tactical missiles (range 75 miles with a nuclear warhead or 45 miles with a conventional payload), and four regiments of artillery equipped with 8-inch and 155-mm howitzers. All nuclear munitions for these systems were held under US custody at Special Ammunition Storage Sites.

In the maritime area the UK in 1980 had four squadrons of Nimrod long-range patrol aircraft capable of delivering American nuclear depth bombs. In addition, two squadrons of nuclear-capable Buccaneer strike/attack aircraft were assigned to SACLANT, along with Royal Navy helicopters — five squadrons of Sea Kings, two flights of Wessex, twenty-five flights of Wasps and eighteen flights of Lynx — all of which were capable of delivering British-designed nuclear depth bombs, providing the bulk of ready theatre nuclear forces in the EASTLANT area. Although final weapon release decisions rested with the UK government, all the above systems were committed to NATO.

In all, the United Kingdom had at its disposal several

hundred strike aircraft and helicopters capable of delivering tactical nuclear weapons, plus the Polaris strategic missiles, but a viable long-range theatre nuclear strike force simply did not exist. The Vulcan force was being progressively run down, the aircraft's operational career having been extended far beyond its planned life, and while the RAF's other nuclear-capable aircraft, such as the Buccaneer, which in 1980 equipped three UK-based squadrons in the maritime attack role and two more in Germany, and the Tornado, which was just coming into service, offered an attack capability that extended from the Murmansk Peninsula southwards to cover much of the Warsaw Pact's territory west of the Soviet border, they were in no sense long-range aircraft, even though their combat radius could be extended by in-flight refuelling.

It was against this background that the United Kingdom agreed to the deployment of Pershing IIs and GLCMs in Europe, and in June 1980 it was confirmed that the GLCMs to be based in the United Kingdom would be deployed at Greenham Common and Molesworth, with six flights housed at Greenham and four at the Cambridgeshire base. The missiles would be stored in special bunkers which would be grass-covered to blend in with the countryside, and no live missiles or warheads would leave the base for the practice deployments that would take place two or three times a month. Such deployments would usually be within a 100-mile radius of the home base, but in time of real war alert there would be no operational reason to limit the area of deployment. As part of the security arrangements, the UK government agreed to contribute 220 British personnel, probably men of the Parachute Regiment or the Royal Air Force Regiment, towards the guard force for the bases and deployment dispersals.

The Ground-Launched Cruise Missile — manufactured by General Dynamics and officially designated BGM-109G — was only one of a family of similar missiles designed to be launched from ships, submarines and aircraft, as well as from land bases, all variants of the General Dynamics BG-109 Tomahawk.

Sea-Launched Cruise Missiles (SLCMs) are deployed aboard the reactivated battleship USS *New Jersey*, and in the mid-1980s there were plans to deploy them on more than 140 cruisers, destroyers and nuclear submarines. There are three versions: the BGM-109A Tactical Land Attack Missile-- Nuclear (TLAM-N) which carries a 200-kiloton W-80 nuclear warhead; the BGM-109B Tactical Anti-Ship Missile (TASM), which carries a 1,000-pound high-explosive warhead and is designed for deployment on submarines; and the BGM-109C Tactical Land Attack Missile-Conventional (TLAM-C), similar to the TLAM-N but with a conventional warhead. The nonnuclear Tomahawks have a range of between 300 and 1,000 miles.

The BGM-109G Ground-Launched Cruise Missile is similar in configuration to the others in the Tomahawk family but has a range of 1,550 miles like the nuclear-armed TLAM-N version and carries the same W-80 nuclear warhead, though other warheads ranging in yield from 10 to 50 kilotons may be fitted depending on operational requirements. All variants are subsonic with a speed of 0.7M (530 mph) at sea level.

In peacetime, GLCM flights are housed in concrete shelters hardened to withstand a direct hit from precision-guided weapons with conventional warheads. Each shelter is divided into three cells, each containing two launch vehicles, and when a GLCM flight is deployed to its war station it travels as two separate elements, each comprising two launchers and a control centre, and the vehicles themselves are armoured against small-arms fire. This is a necessary precaution, for in time of war cruise missile sites and launch vehicles en route would come under attack by agents of Spetsnaz, the Soviet Special Forces.

The first of ninety-six GLCMs destined for Greenham Common arrived on 14 November 1983 aboard a C-141B Starlifter, which was placed under heavy guard by USAF and RAF police and British paratroops while the rounds were offloaded and transported to their shelters. (Deployment at Molesworth, the other UK base, was scheduled to begin in 1987.) Command and support of the missiles at Greenham Common is the responsibility of the 501st Tactical Missile Wing, which is subordinate to the Third Air Force.

The cruise missile's transporter/erector/launcher is a

78,000-pound cross-country vehicle comprising a semi-trailer with an elevating armoured launcher containing four GLCM rounds towed by an MAN tractor. The launch control centre is a similar cross-country vehicle with a semi-trailer mounting an armoured shelter and generators. Each GLCM flight has a primary and backup control centre linked by fibre-optic, electromagnetic pulse-resistant cable. (EMP is the massive burst of energy released by a nuclear explosion; it can cause severe damage to communications, radars and so forth.)

In the event of a war alert the 501st TMW's cruise missiles could be deployed to pre-surveyed sites almost anywhere in southern England and as far west as the Welsh border. Once the missiles are on site, planning for their nuclear mission needs about an hour, during which the weapons remain vulnerable to Spetsnaz commandos. The Theatre Mission Planning System allows the operator to select appropriate waypoints and Terrain Contour Matching (TERCOM) maps, which enable the missile to avoid enemy defences en route to its target. The TERCOM system would not have been possible without years of satellite reconnaissance, which has produced highly accurate, detailed and constantly updated terrain maps of both friendly and potentially hostile territory. The information from the satellite photographs is digitized and stored in the cruise missile's computer.

Once the cruise missile is launched, it is guided by inertial navigation, updated at intervals to eliminate drift errors by means of the missile's radar altimeter, a part of the guidance system which enables the missile to maintain smooth, terrain-hugging flight at altitudes down to 200 feet. (The idea is by no means new. Britain's own Blue Steel missile, carried by Vulcans and Victors in the 1960s, also used an inertial navigation system which was linked with that of the parent aircraft, providing additional information to the crew on their position and, by comparing data obtained from fixes along the route, enabling corrections to be fed into the missile.)

The continuous stream of height data supplied by the radar altimeter is used to produce a profile of the ground over which the missile is flying and, by comparing this with stored data, to update the inertial platform. TERCOM maps are composed of matrices of spot heights drawn by the US Defense Mapping Agency and loaded into the missile's memory before launch. As the GLCM flies over a TERCOM field its altimeter maps the ground directly below and the data is compared with that in the stored matrix. The flight path is identified and checked against the pre-planned route, and commands to rectify any errors are transmitted to the autopilot. By comparing three consecutive TERCOM fixes within the field, the possibility of the flight path being wrongly updated is eliminated.

As the flight progresses the TERCOM maps become smaller and more detailed until the terminal matrix is reached just before the target, when final adjustments are made to the missile's flight path. Each potential target is surrounded by several terminal matrices, allowing the launch controller to choose the direction of attack and, if necessary, to arrange for several missiles to arrive on target from different directions.

The missile's memory contains up to twenty TERCOM maps. Between the TERCOM fields the GLCM navigates by means of pre-programmed, time-related waypoints, flying between them in straight lines at speeds and altitudes determined before launch. The pre-designated route takes advantage of local terrain for concealment, avoids known defences and is designed to disguise its true destination.

Suppose, for example, that a GLCM launched from southern England had the big Soviet naval base of Kronshtadt, at the eastern end of the Gulf of Finland, as its target. Its route might take it out over the North Sea to make landfall on the Norwegian coast near Bergen, where its inertial navigation system would set it on course to the first TERCOM field, on the border between Norway and Sweden; from there it might turn south to fly through the Swedish valleys to a second TERCOM field at Lake Vänern, cruising on at 200 feet to cross the Swedish coast near Norrköping and enter the Baltic Sea, before continuing between the islands of Oland and Gotland to another TERCOM field on the Gulf of Danzig.

From then on the GLCM would be over enemy territory, manoeuvring to avoid known air defence sites and swinging north across Poland and Lithuania to pass well to the landward of the Gulf of Riga and enter its final TERCOM fields. As well as SAM and AAA sites it would now have to run the gauntlet of early warning aircraft and interceptors armed with snap-down missiles; but being made of materials with a low radar signature it would be extremely difficult to detect, and the odds would be on it reaching its objective. (To increase its chances of survival, the missile would probably be launched at night, when its radar guidance would be unaffected, but air activity would be greatly reduced.)

The hypothetical GLCM flight profile described above involves it entering the neutral airspace of Sweden, but nuclear wars are no respecters of neutrality and such a route would be quite probable. In fact, likely routes might lie anywhere from Norway in the north to the Swiss border in the south, and would take cruise missiles to targets as far south as Odessa and as far north as Murmansk. The missile would be programmed to pop up at the end of its approach before diving on its target in a manoeuvre designed to circumvent any barriers, such as cables or high earthworks, that might be built to protect important targets against horizontal attack.

Despite its sophistication, the viability of the GLCM — by comparison with the air- and sea-launched versions — remains questionable. It takes time to deploy and its bases are consequently vulnerable to surprise attack; and while such an attack by enemy land-based missiles would be virtually impossible to mount because of intelligence and other indications, submarine-launched ballistic missiles such as the USA's Trident II, and presumably the latest generation of comparable Soviet weapons, have a Circular Error Probable of only 120 metres, which makes them effective against hard targets such as command bunkers and missile silos. They could, as a result, conceivably be used as first-strike weapons against purely military objectives.

To escape annihilation in such a surprise attack GLCMs would have to be deployed to their war stations at a very early stage in any serious rise in international tension. They would also have to be used first, because in no sense is the cruise missile a retaliatory weapon. But neither were the NATO tactical nuclear weapons that preceded them; the option to use them first has always existed as part of the flexible response doctrine.

In this respect the deployment of GLCMs in Britain and elsewhere in Europe does not deviate at all from previous NATO policy; rather it bridges the crucial gap opened up in the 1970s by the deployment of new Soviet weaponry — no more and no less.

However, the deployment of cruise missiles in Europe has introduced another factor which, in the long term, could prove to be the most important of all: it has made the whole question of nuclear weapons policy an issue for public debate for the first time since the early 1960s. This time, the public are insisting on their right to know what is happening in their midst, and they will doubtless continue to do so.

10

The Men and Women of 'Little America'

DURING THE FORTY-ODD years since its return to postwar Britain, the United States Air Force has had its share of publicity, both good and bad. What is extraordinary, however, is that the average British citizen knows next to nothing about the USAF personnel and their families who inhabit those sprawling bases. Those who do know display reactions varying from love to hate — one of the haters rather uncharitably described our US allies as 'Russians with creases in their trousers' — but whatever one feels about the Americans it is quite impossible to ignore them. After four decades they are a fact of British life.

From the British point of view, it is perhaps a little hurtful to be classed as natives and foreigners by people who bear British names and speak the English language. Nevertheless, the USAF public relations machine goes to considerable lengths to keep things sweet between hosts and tenants, beginning with a very thorough briefing and by issuing a booklet called *Welcome to Britain* to families arriving here for the first time. Each base also has a UK Community Relations Adviser, appointed by the Ministry of Defence, whose task is to smooth out any problems between the Americans and the locals.

Most of the problems occur when newly-arrived families rent or buy accommodation off-base. Americans are used to open-plan gardens, and it takes time and patience to teach children that they are not supposed to clamber over other people's hedges and fences or trample over their flower beds. The Briton's traditional desire for privacy is something many Americans find hard to understand at first, but eventually most come to like it too.

Life on the air bases is so containerised and self-sufficient that some families hardly ever leave their precincts throughout a three-year tour of duty. Because of accommodation problems, however, many families are forced to live off-base, and there are very few indeed who fail to involve themselves with the local community. At least one man has even given his life for it.

In 1963 Colonel Wendell J. Kelley was deputy commander of the 20th Tactical Fighter Wing, then flying F-100 Super Sabres from Wethersfield. Kelley, who was forty-three, lived off-base with his wife and three children in the nearby village of Gosfield, where he was deeply involved in a number of local activities to do with youngsters and had played a big part in raising funds for a new village playing field.

On the morning of 23 January 1963 Kelley took off from Wethersfield in a two-seat F-100F on an instrument training sortie over southern England; the pilot he was checking out was twenty-five-year-old First Lieutenant Paul Briggs.

Half way into the sortie, when they were at 30,000 feet north of London, there was an explosion in the F-100's engine, followed by a loss of power. The aircraft was still under control, so Kelley put out an emergency call and received a radar steer to the Blackwater Estuary, where he jettisoned the Super Sabre's underwing fuel tanks. Anglia Control then gave him a heading for Wethersfield and he turned towards base, the aircraft descending slowly under reduced engine power. Anglia Control brought him down through the cloud layer to position his aircraft for a straight-in approach to Wethersfield's main runway.

Both pilots knew that as long as they had a margin of power available they would be able to make the airfield, but while they were still in cloud the worst happened: there was another explosion and the engine flamed out. Kelley tried to re-start it, but it had seized solid.

The Super Sabre broke through the cloud base at 6,000 feet; at 4,500 feet it still had six or seven miles to go, and there was now no possibility of reaching the runway: with a dead engine the heavy aircraft would be at zero altitude in five miles or less. While Briggs kept the F-100 on its glide path, Kelley made further attempts to relight the engine, but without success.

Calmly, he told Wethersfield's approach controller that he intended to turn the aircraft towards a clear spot where both pilots could eject.

On the ground, eye-witnesses saw the Super Sabre alter course several times to take it clear of the little town of Halstead and the scattered villages that lay in its path. With the altitude down to 1,500 feet Kelley ordered Briggs to eject. The younger pilot did so successfully, but Kelley remained at the controls as the aircraft, becoming increasingly unstable, descended towards Gosfield, where Kelley had made his home. At 200 mph the jet plunged into a nearby field and exploded; Kelley had made no attempt to eject.

A few days later, more than 250 villagers braved the worst snowdrifts they could remember to attend a memorial service for Colonel Kelley at Wethersfield. They were convinced that the pilot had deliberately sacrificed his own chances of survival by staying at the controls to ensure that the plunging aircraft missed the homes of the people who had become his friends.

The same kind of skill and professionalism had earlier been displayed by two more 20th TFW pilots, this time with a happier outcome. On 23 October 1957 Lieutenants Ray Krasovich and Billy Ray of the 55th Fighter-Bomber Squadron, which had recently converted to F-100s, took off from Wethersfield on a two-ship training sortie over the North Sea. As they rejoined formation after practising some individual manoeuvres, Ray — momentarily blinded by the sun — collided with Krasovich's Super Sabre, damaging its rear fuselage and buckling its tail, while his own aircraft lost two feet of its nose, together with the Pitot tube. Without this his airspeed indicator ceased to function, which would present a critical and possibly fatal problem during the approach to land. Nevertheless, both aircraft were still handling adequately, and Krasovich decided to accompany Ray's F-100 right down to the runway threshold so that the other pilot could match his approach speed.

'That nose out in front there looked awful odd,' Ray said later, 'but Kraz made a real good job of bringing me in. I could hear the GCA (Ground Controlled Approach) instructions through my headphones and always, just when I would normally have glanced at the clock, Kraz broke in with the airspeed. We broke cloud. I was right up level with Kraz's wing and we were both nicely lined up with the runway. He took me right down to approach speed and up to the end of the runway. Few pilots need their ASI after that — they just feel the aircraft down.'

With Ray safely over the runway threshold and within yards of touchdown, Krasovich broke away and climbed back into the circuit. He knew that it would be dangerous to have two damaged aircraft careering down the runway at the same time, and he had also noticed that his own aircraft's damaged tail was causing handling problems at low speed. Accordingly, he flew around for a while to get the feel of the F-100 at low speeds before making his own approach to land, which he accomplished successfully.

Super Sabre pilots were the first to admit that without power the aircraft's gliding qualities were akin to those of a brick. One aircraft, though, was worse: the F-101 Voodoo; and it was in an F-101 that Captain Jack E. Shephard of the 91st Tactical Fighter Squadron, 81st TFW, found himself presented with a very unenviable situation during a sortie from Bentwaters in October 1960. Shephard was returning to base after a two-hour practice bombing sortie over France; the weather was bad and he positioned himself over the North Sea for a GCA approach, turning left towards the coast and the instrument runway at his home airfield. At 1,800 feet, with everything going smoothly and the voice of the GCA controller holding the Voodoo nicely on the glide path, Shephard closed the throttles to lose speed prior to lowering his undercarriage; with the landing gear down and locked he went to push open the twin throttle levers again, and it was then that his problems began: the levers refused to budge.

The Voodoo was down to 1,400 feet now, and if its sink rate remained unchecked it would crash on the Suffolk coast in less than sixty seconds. At first Shephard thought that the throttle levers had moved but that there must be some problem with the fuel system, so more valuable seconds were wasted while he tried switching tanks, and by the time he realised that the levers themselves were causing the trouble his aircraft was passing through 1,000 feet.

Shephard considered ejecting, but the prospect of plunging into the icy North Sea was far from appealing. Moreover, he was appalled by the thought of the Voodoo plummeting down somewhere on the quiet coastline, perhaps causing civilian casualties. Releasing his safety harness, he managed to get his left foot behind the throttle levers and shoved with all his strength. He was fighting for his own life now; with his harness undone he could not eject, and he would not have enough time to strap himself in again before his aircraft reached too low an altitude.

Over the R-T, the GCA controller's voice was becoming more and more urgent as he saw the Voodoo's blip sinking lower on his radar screen, but Shephard was too busy trying to move the throttle levers to use the radio. Still pushing desperately hard with his foot, he finally felt one of the levers budge a little — not much, but enough to restore some vital engine power. Slowly, the heavy fighter-bomber began to climb back on to the glide path.

Shephard dared not take his foot off the lever, because as soon as he did so it snapped back into the closed position again, and the Voodoo went down the glide path in a kind of porpoising motion, its engine power surging when he pushed the throttle lever and falling away again as soon as he relaxed the pressure. Fortunately, because both its engines were close to fuselage centreline, the Voodoo suffered no serious asymmetric flying problems, so Shephard had no need to take his foot off the throttle lever to operate the rudder pedals.

The Voodoo broke cloud a mile short of the runway, and Shephard saw at once that he was too low. Power came on as he shoved the throttle lever again, but it was not enough, and in desperation he cut in the afterburner, gaining additional thrust to take him over the last few hundred yards. As the runway threshold passed below him he at last moved his aching foot from the lever and the aircraft sank to the concrete as the power died away. The brake parachute popped out and the Voodoo rolled to a stop undamaged, thanks to a very fine feat of airmanship.

To the Third Air Force, the mission — in other words, maintaining the combat force ready to go to war at very short notice — is all-important, and no effort is spared to support the operational task. Ground crews work round the clock in eight-hour shifts to keep the aircraft on top line, a task that involves a high proportion of women. Flying training is intensive and constant, and there is an inevitable quota of accidents.

Until comparatively recently the USAF — and indeed the RAF — have been reluctant to reveal details of military aircraft accidents for security reasons, but following severe media criticism of military accident rates brief details began to be published from the beginning of 1979. An examination of the Third Air Force's accident figures from January 1979 to December 1984 shows that most of the losses involved F-111s, often as a consequence of their low-level role.

The following list gives details of USAF aircraft lost while operating from UK bases but does not include Third Air Force aircraft lost while deployed overseas; a number of F-5E aggressor aircraft from Alconbury were destroyed accidentally during air combat training in various NATO countries, for example, as were some 81st TFW A-10 Thunderbolt IIs deployed to forward locations in Germany.

1979
28 March   RF-4C Phantom of the 10th TRW, Alconbury, crashed through unknown causes at Newton Steward, Scotland; two crew killed.
20 April   Two F-111Fs of the 48th TFW, Lakenheath, collided during practice bombing run at Tain, Scotland; both crews ejected safely.
27 April   RF-4C Phantom of the 10th TRW crashed on the North Yorkshire Moors near Whitby following engine fire at low level; both crew members were killed. (It was believed that the pilot had remained at the controls to steer the aircraft clear of buildings.)
7 July   A-10 of the 81st TFW crashed near Chicksands during an air display; pilot killed.
24 July   F-111E of the 20th TFW, Upper Heyford, crashed into the sea off Hull through unknown causes; both crew killed.
30 October   F-111E of the 20th TFW crashed near

Cambridge during a low-level sortie at night; both crew members escaped.

12 December   F-111E of the 20th TFW missing over the North Sea in the Wash area, together with both crew members.

19 December   F-111E of the 20th TFW crashed in the Glen Trool area of southwest Scotland near Newton Stewart after completing a practice bombing mission on the Jurby Range, Isle of Man; both crew members killed.

1980

29 April   F-111E of the 20th TFW crashed near Wareham; both crew killed.

1981

9 January   A-10 of the 81st TFW crashed off Donna Nook, Lincolnshire, during a live firing sortie; pilot killed.

2 February   F-111F of the 48th TFW crashed at East Wretham, Norfolk, on the approach to land at Lakenheath; both crew members escaped.

25 March   F-111E of the 20th TFW lost power on takeoff from RAF Fairford, sank back onto the runway, overran the end and was badly damaged; both crew escaped.

8 May   A-10 of the 81st TFW crashed at Wainfleet, Lincolnshire, during live firing sortie. The pilot ejected but the altitude of the aircraft was outside the seat's envelope and his parachute failed to deploy. He was picked up by an RAF Sea King helicopter but died in hospital.

1982

23 June   F-111F of the 48th TFW crashed near Porin, Scotland, after being abandoned by its crew following a violent and uncontrollable pitch-up; both crew members survived.

16 September   F-111F of the 48th TFW crashed through unknown causes near RAF Leuchars, Scotland; both crew survived.

1 November   F-111F of the 48th TFW crashed in southern Turkey during a training sortie from the UK; both crew members escaped.

7 December   F-111F of the 48th TFW crashed into a mountain on the Isle of Skye; both crew members killed.

1983
26 April   F-111F of the 48th TFW crashed into the North Sea during a low-level sortie in bad weather; both crew killed.
6 June   RF-4C of the 10th TRW, Alconbury, crashed at Oudeschip in the Netherlands following loss of control during a low-level sortie; both crew members ejected safely.
12 December   Two A-10s of the 81st TFW lost after a mid-air collision off East Anglia; one pilot killed, the other rescued.
21 December   F-111F of the 48th TFW abandoned over the North Sea after loss of control; both crew members rescued.

1984
9 August   F-111E of the 20th TFW crashed in Loch Eye, Scotland, during a low-level sortie; crew ejected safely.

One accident has been deliberately omitted from this list because it highlights the dangers experienced by the air-sea rescue crews of the RAF and USAF, men of great courage and skill whose exploits deserve at least one tribute in this book. On 18 November 1980 two A-10s of the 81st TFW were involved in a mid-air collision while en route from Bentwaters to Wainfleet Range on the northern shore of the Wash; the aircraft were flying at between 1,500 and 2,000 feet, and the collision occurred at 09.15 hours.

The pilot of one A-10, Major Steve Kaatz, lost control of his aircraft following the collision and ejected safely; the aircraft crashed near the village of Itteringham in Norfolk, and an off-duty air traffic controller from Norwich Airport was slightly injured by flying debris from the aircraft. The pilot of the other A-10, Lieutenant-Colonel William Olson, attempted a return to Bentwaters by flying round the Norfolk coastline to avoid built-up areas, but he lost control and was forced to eject, coming down in the sea off Winterton.

The duty search and rescue crew of C Flight, No. 202 Squadron, RAF, were alerted at 09.24 and their Sea King helicopter took off from RAF Coltishall at 09.34 to pick up Major Kaatz at Itteringham. Six minutes later, while en route to the crash site, the Sea King crew were diverted to rescue Colonel Olson, arriving over him at 09.45. The American pilot was still in his parachute and was being dragged through the water a few miles from Winterton; it was not clear to the helicopter crew at this stage whether he was conscious or not. He was drifting in waves between ten and fifteen feet high, whipped up by a wind that was gusting up to forty knots.

The RAF winchman, Master Air Loadmaster Dave Bullock — who was thirty-eight years old and had spent twenty-two years in the RAF, three of them on search and rescue work — went down to free the pilot from his parachute. During the operation he somehow became entangled in the parachute lines, and the combined weight of the two men and the water-logged parachute snapped the winch cable, which was normally capable of resisting a stress of 3,700 pounds. MALM Bullock and Colonel Olson were then dragged along by the parachute, which was blowing before the gale-force wind.

Because of the sea state there was no possibility of the Sea King's pilot attempting a landing on the water. All he could do was follow the dragging parachute and home in a USAF HH-53 helicopter from the 67th Aerospace Rescue and Recovery Squadron at RAF Woodbridge which had taken off at 09.47, just after the Sea King had been diverted to pick up Colonel Olson. Guided by the Sea King, the American helicopter dropped two para-rescue men into the water to deflate and cut free the parachute from the winchman and pilot; the drop was made about 25 minutes after the HH-53 took off, and the para-rescue men, in full skindiving kit including oxygen bottles, succeeded in cutting Bullock and Olson free. Both men were taken on board the HH-53, but tragically were pronounced dead on arrival at Norwich.

The winchman fatality was the only one in the thirty-year history of search and rescue helicopter operations in the United Kingdom, and the only known case in which a winch cable had snapped.

It might be thought that the deaths of Dave Bullock and Bill

General Dynamics F-111Fs of the 48th Tactical Fighter Wing, RAF Lakenheath. The F-111F can penetrate deep into enemy territory at low level in all weathers, carrying either nuclear or conventional war loads.

Pressure waves stream back over a 48th TFW F-111's wings as it streaks at low level over Loch Ness during a training sortie from Lakenheath.

Latest member of the F-111 family is the EF-111 Raven, developed by Grumman Aircraft for electronic countermeasures and jamming. Twelve aircraft of this type equip the 42nd Electronic Combat Squadron at Upper Heyford, the first having been delivered in February 1984. In war, Ravens would accompany F-111s on their low-level penetration missions, jamming enemy radars.

Olson were needless — indeed, that the accidental death of anyone engaged in military flying is pointless. But while the barriers between East and West continue to exist, the price of liberty will remain constant vigilance; and sometimes that vigilance will exact its own high price in the lives of brave men.

APPENDIX

United States Air Force Bases in Britain, 1945–85

ALCONBURY (Huntingdon)

After being relinquished by the RAF on 26 November 1945, Alconbury remained inactive until 1 June 1953, when it was reactivated by the USAF. The first unit to move in was the 7523rd Air Base Squadron, which set about extending the existing installations to receive the first combat squadrons. This work received fresh impetus in 1954 when the main runway was lengthened, and in March 1955 the 7560th Air Base Group moved in to pave the way for the arrival, on 15 September 1955, of the 85th Bomb Squadron from Sculthorpe with its B-45 Tornados. The 85th, which was later equipped with Douglas B-66Bs, remained at Alconbury until August 1959, when it was replaced by the 1st and 30th Squadrons of the 10th Tactical Reconnaissance Wing from Spangdahlem, Germany. Shortly before the 85th's departure, the airfield was occupied briefly, from May to August 1959, by the WB-50Ds of the 53rd Weather Squadron. The 10th Tactical Reconnaissance Wing operated RB-66s out of Alconbury until May 1965, when the Wing began to re-equip with RF-4C Phantom IIs.

The 1st Tactical Reconnaissance Squadron still operates RF-4Cs, the 30th TRS having been deactivated on 1 April 1976. May of that year saw the formation at Alconbury of the is also used by the 17th Tactical Reconnaissance Wing, operating TR-1 battlefield surveillance aircraft, and by the US Army on a regular basis for helicopter operations.

AYR (Strathclyde)

Ayr airfield, which was closed in 1946 after wartime use as an armament practice camp and naval air station, reopened in 1951 and was used until 1977 as a storage site in support of USAF units at Prestwick.

BASSINGBOURN (Cambridgeshire)

In the years following the Second World War Bassingbourn was used by squadrons of RAF Transport Command, but on 25 August 1950, as a result of heightened international tension following the outbreak of the Korean War, the B-29 Superfortresses of the 353rd Bomb Squadron, 301st Bomb Group, were deployed here on overseas detachment. Because of the international situation this unit remained at Bassingbourn until January 1951, when it was replaced by the RB-50Bs of the 38th Squadron, 55th Strategic Reconnaissance Wing, which stayed until May 1951, when they were in turn replaced on a rotation basis by the B-50Ds of the 97th Bomb Group. With the departure of the 97th in September 1951 Bassingbourn reverted to RAF control.

BENTWATERS (Suffolk)

Having been an RAF jet fighter station in the years immediately after the war, Bentwaters was inactive from 1 September 1949 until 1 July 1950, when it was placed under Care and Maintenance and eventually transferred to the USAF on 16 March 1951. Six months later, on 3 September 1951, the 91st Squadron of the 81st Fighter Interceptor Group arrived with their F-86A Sabres, the first aircraft of this kind to be based in

Europe. On 1 April 1954 the Group was redesignated the 81st Fighter-Bomber Wing and began to replace its Sabres with F-84F Thunderstreaks, the re-equipment being completed by January 1955. On 8 July 1958 the unit was redesignated the 81st Tactical Fighter Wing, and shortly afterwards it received the first examples of a potent new long-range tactical fighter, the McDonnell F-101 Voodoo: by the end of the year the Wing had received its full complement of these aircraft and its forty-one F-84Fs were then transferred to the Federal German Luftwaffe. The 81st TFW now comprised the 91st and 92nd Squadrons, the latter having arrived from Manston in April.

In October 1965 the Wing received the first examples of the F-4C Phantom II, and by April 1966 was fully equipped with these aircraft. The Wing's third squadron, the 78th TFS, at Woodbridge, re-equipped with F-4D Phantoms in the summer of 1969, and the 91st and 92nd Squadrons at Bentwaters also received F-4Ds in September 1973. In the autumn of 1978 the 81st TFW's Phantoms began to be replaced by A-10 Thunderbolts and today the Wing maintains forward operating locations in West Germany, aircraft being sent out from either Bentwaters or Woodbridge in clutches of eight. Squadrons based at Bentwaters in 1985 were the 92nd, 509th, 510th and 511th Tactical Fighter Squadrons with the 78th and 91st Tactical Fighter Squadrons at Woodbridge.

BOVINGDON (Hertfordshire)

Bovingdon, an important USAAF bomber base during the Second World War, was subsequently used by BOAC and BEA for a period of five years, after which it returned to American use on 25 May 1951, the USAF unit involved being the 7531st Air Base Squadron operating C-47 transports. Bovingdon remained in American hands until 1962, serving as a communications base for the US Third Air Division HQ at South Ruislip, and a wide variety of American aircraft types visited the base during this period. They included most types of transports on the USAF inventory, as well as occasional visitors such as the B-29, B-50, and B-26. After the departure of the

Americans, Bovingdon passed under the control of the RAF's
Southern Communications Squadron.

BRIZE NORTON (Oxfordshire)

For fifteen years Brize Norton was one of the most important
USAF bases in Britain. After reconstruction of the runways
and airfield installations the base was officially handed over to
the USAF on 16 April 1951, and the first American bombers
were deployed here on 27 June 1952 in the form of twenty-one
B-36Ds and B-36Fs of the 11th Bomb Wing (H), Carswell Air
Force Base; their deployment was only temporary, and they
flew out again a fortnight later. Regular deployments to Brize
Norton by Strategic Air Command units under the control of
the 7503rd Strategic Wing began in December 1952 with the
arrival of B-29s of the 301st Bomb Wing; this unit remained
until March 1953 when it was replaced by the B-50As of the
65th Squadron, 43rd Bomb Wing.

   The deployment of the 301st BW to Brize Norton and also to
Fairford, Greenham Common and Upper Heyford, was a stop-
gap measure pending the arrival of the first B-47 Stratojets:
these arrived in September 1953 with two squadrons of the
305th Bomb Wing from Limestone AFB, Maine. B-47 detachments during the months that followed were from the 22nd
BW, the 320th BW, and the 43rd BW, and to extend the
periods of continuous Airborne Alert flown as a matter of
routine by the Stratojets the KC-97Gs of the 321st Air Refuelling Squadron arrived in December 1944, followed by similar
aircraft of the 310th Air Refuelling Squadron.

   SAC detachments continued until September 1955, when
Brize Norton closed for six months to undergo runway repairs,
and the next SAC unit to move in was the 307th BW, again with
B-47s, followed in January 1957 by the 384th BW. January 16
1957 saw the arrival in Britain of the first B-52B Stratofortress,
an aircraft of the 93rd BW which touched down after a flight
from Castle Air Force Base in California. The next SAC Unit to
arrive, in April 1957, was the 380th BW with B-47Es, and its
departure was followed by another period of airfield closure for

runway repair. B-47 units deployed to Brize Norton early in 1958 included the 68th Bomb Wing and a squadron of the 100th BW. From March 1958 the KC-97G tankers which had accompanied the SAC detachments began to be replaced by KC-135s.

In April 1958 six B-52Ds of the 92nd BW were deployed to Brize Norton to take part in the annual Anglo-American bomber competition and B-52s continued to visit the airfield at irregular intervals. By this time Strategic Air Command's policy of sending its bombers overseas on three-month deployments had changed, small groups of aircraft now being deployed on Reflex Alert which rendered the overseas bases less crowded and vulnerable. During this period RB-47s of the 55th and 98th Strategic Reconnaissance Wings also visited Brize Norton, together with the occasional U-2 en route to or from clandestine missions over the Soviet Union. The airfield was occasionally visited by B-58 Hustlers from January 1964, but the days of Brize Norton as a USAF base were numbered: the last SAC bomber, a B-47E of the 330th BW, flew out on 3 April 1965 and the airfield subsequently reverted to RAF use.

BRUNTINGTHORPE (Leicestershire)

Bruntingthorpe's career as a USAF base was brief. Although it was allocated to USAF use in November 1953, it reverted to Air Ministry control at the end of that year and was not reallocated to the USAF until February 1957. A new runway, suitable for high-performance jets, was built and Bruntingthorpe was designated as a satellite airfield for RAF Alconbury, the first unit to move in being the 3912th Air Base Squadron. January 1959 saw the start of a ninety-day rotation period by the B-47s of Strategic Air Command's 100th Bomb Wing; these were followed in August by the RB-66Bs of the 19th Tactical Reconnaissance Squadron, 10th TRW, which remained until the autumn of 1962. Bruntingthorpe, which featured regular SAC deployments until that time, then closed as an airfield.

BURTONWOOD (Cheshire)

Burtonwood, an important USAAF supply and maintenance base during the Second World War, was re-opened for USAF use in 1948 as a supply depot for Strategic Air Command Units on detachment to the United Kingdom. During the Berlin Airlift Burtonwood was responsible for the inspection and overhaul of C-54 transport aircraft, and afterwards the base retained its responsibility for the maintenance of aircraft and supply of material to USAF airfields in Britain, being designated the Northern Air Material Area on 1 September 1953. Burtonwood's resident unit was the 53rd Weather Reconnaissance Squadron, with WB-50s, but the base was visited by almost every aircraft type in USAF service from time to time, including — in 1956 — a detachment of B-36 bombers. Up to 1958 Burtonwood had been the main terminal for the Military Air Transport Service in the United Kingdom, but this now moved to Mildenhall and the WB-50s of the 53rd WRS went to Alconbury. With the departure of the United States Forces from France Burtonwood became a massive storage complex, and today, together with Caerwent in South Wales, it is the main storage facility for US weaponry in the UK.

CHELVESTON (Northamptonshire)

Chelveston, from where USAAF B-17s had operated from 1942 to 1945, returned to American control in December 1952 with the arrival of the 3914th Air Base Group, Strategic Air Command. For the next few years Chelveston was the scene of frequent SAC B-47 deployments, but the only resident flying unit was the 42nd Tactical Reconnaissance Squadron, 10th Tactical Reconnaissance Wing, which arrived from Spangdahlem in August 1959 with its RB-66s and remained until August 1962. Chelveston subsequently became a reserve airfield and the site of the USAF communications and storage centre.

CHICKSANDS (Bedfordshire)

In 1985 RAF Chicksands, near Shefford, was the site of a US Air Force electronic security command station under the control of the 7274th Air Base Group, Third Air Force, USAFE.

EAST KIRKBY (Lincolnshire)

In the early 1950s, as part of the programme to provide additional facilities for the United States Air Forces in Europe, East Kirkby was substantially modernised and in August 1954 the C-47s of the 3917th Air Base Squadron of SAC's 7th Air Division flew in. This unit remained until 1958, when the airfield reverted to RAF use before its eventual closure.

ELVINGTON (Yorkshire)

After a period under the control of RAF Maintenance Command, Elvington was allocated to the USAF in June 1953 as part of the expansion of SAC's overseas bases. The airfield was completely modernised, with new runways laid and installations erected, at enormous cost, but it was never used for its intended purpose: the Americans departed in December 1958 and Elvington was subsequently used as a relief landing ground for RAF Flying Training Schools in the Vale of York.

FAIRFORD (Gloucestershire)

Work on enlarging Fairford and extending its facilities began with American help in the summer of 1950, and on 1 July 1951 in the base came under the control of the 7th Air Division, Strategic Air Command. During the next eighteen months the airfield was visited by detachments of B-29s and B-50s, and then, on 7 February 1953 seventeen B-36 bombers arrived from Carswell Air Force Base, Texas. A few weeks later, on 7 April, two B-47 Stratojets landed at Fairford; this was a preliminary to the arrival on 2 June, of the 367th, 368th and 369th Squadrons of the 306th Bomb Wing, whose B-47Bs stayed until 4 September 1953. In addition to the regular B-47 detachments that arrived at Fairford during the succeeding months, usually in the form of a single squadron, the base also saw detachments by the RB-47Es of the 68th Strategic Reconnaissance Wing and the RB-36Fs of the 5th Strategic Reconnaissance Wing, both of which occupied Fairford for some weeks in 1954. The use of Fairford by Strategic Air Command continued until the early 1960s, although on a much reduced scale, and the airfield reverted to RAF use in June 1964. Fairford, however, still maintains a USAF flight refuelling facility, and is used by the KC-135s of the 34th and 922nd Strategic Squadrons of the 11th Strategic Group, SAC.

FOULSHAM (Norfolk)

Foulsham was briefly occupied by the USAF in 1954-55, when a special signals unit was based there. The airfield subsequently ceased to have a military use.

FULL SUTTON (Yorkshire)

After being relinquished by the RAF in 1954 Full Sutton was designated a reserve site for the US Air Force from 1955 to 1957, but it was never used operationally. However, the 3930th Air Base Squadron, SAC, was based there during that period to provide support for SAC deployments to Elvington, which in the event never took place.

GREENHAM COMMON (Berkshire)

Greenham Common's long association with the United States Air Force began in April 1951, when an extensive airfield re-building programme was begun by the 804th Engineer Aviation Battalion, the base's administration being taken over by the 7501st Air Base Squadron. Wartime installations were destroyed and a new 10,000-foot east-west runway was laid. The airfield was formally handed over from nominal Air Ministry control to the 7th Air Division, 3rd Air Force, USAFE in June 1951, but the reconstruction work was not completed until September 1953, when the base was declared operationally ready to receive B-47 Stratojets.

The first operational deployment to Greenham Common by Strategic Air Command took place in March 1954 and involved a detachment of the 303rd Bomb Wing's B-47s. Their stay, however, was short, for the runway showed signs of breaking up and the 303rd had to move to Fairford to complete its deployment. In April 1956, following extensive runway repairs, Greenham Common passed under the control of the 3909th Air Base Group and shortly afterwards the 97th Air Refuelling Squadron arrived with KC-97G tankers. In October 1956 the 310th Bomb Wing arrived with forty-five B-47s, whose operations caused a considerable outcry among the local population, and public opposition to the use of Greenham intensified in March 1958 when a B-47 was forced to jettison its underwing fuel tanks following engine failure on takeoff; one tank exploded inside a hangar and the other hit a parked B-47, causing a fire that raged for several hours and destroyed another B-47 that was parked close by.

In April 1958 the ninety-day deployments came to an end and were replaced by three-week Reflex Alert rotations, which considerably reduced the noise factor. In the early 1960s Greenham Common was the scene of periodic visits by B-52 Stratofortress bombers, and on one occasion, in October 1963, by a B-58 Hustler, but the only regular Strategic Air Command visitors continued to be B-47s on Reflex Alert. These deployments continued until April 1964, when a change in USAF policy resulted in the airfield being handed back to RAF control three months later.

In the late 1960s Greenham Common was designated a NATO standby base under the control of the 7551st Combat Support Group and was subsequently used as the terminal for a number of rapid reinforcement exercises. In March 1976 the 20th Tactical Fighter Wing's F-111Es moved in from Upper

Heyford for three months while that airfield's runways were resurfaced. Later plans to use Greenham Common as a base for KC-135A tankers were never implemented, largely due to local opposition, and although an American presence remained there in the form of the 7273rd Air Base Group from 1979 the airfield passed briefly out of the news. Then came a renewed outcry; in June 1980 it was announced that Greenham Common was to be one of two sites in Britain where US cruise missiles were to be deployed. The first of these weapons, operated by the 11th Tactical Missile Squadron of the 501st Tactical Missile Wing, arrived at Greenham in May 1983 aboard C-5A Galaxys.

KIRKNEWTON (Lothian)

Kirknewton, a former RAF maintenance unit, was used for storage in the 1950s by the 7535th Air Base Squadron, USAF, but reverted to RAF control in 1967. It subsequently became the home of No. 661 Air Cadet Gliding School.

LAKENHEATH (Suffolk)

Lakenheath has remained one of the most important USAF bases in Britain for four decades. The initial American presence here involved B-29s of the 2nd Bomb Group, which arrived in July 1948 in response to growing international tension over the Russian blockade of Berlin. During the next ten years the base was visited by more than thirty Strategic Air Command units on ninety-day operational deployments, the B-29s giving way in August 1949 to B-50As supported by their KB-29M tankers.

The first B-50A unit to visit Lakenheath was the 65th Bomb Squadron, 43rd Bomb Group, and from January 1951 SAC deployments also involved B-36Ds supported by C-124 Globemasters carrying spares and ground crew. During the next few months Lakenheath became the principal base for USAF strategic reconnaissance activities in the United Kingdom and was frequently used by detachments of RB-36s and

RB-50s. The first B-47s visited Lakenheath in April 1953 but operational deployments by these aircraft did not begin until June the following year, when supporting KC-97 tankers were also based here. In 1956 there was much local speculation when a mysterious jet aircraft with long glider-like wings was seen slipping into and out of Lakenheath; it was subsequently identified as a Lockheed U-2. Later that year the base was vacated by the Americans, but they returned in January 1960 with the arrival of the 48th Tactical Fighter Wing from France. The unit successively operated F-100D Super Sabres, F-4 Phantoms, and F-111Fs, which were still Lakenheath's tenants in 1985.

LINDHOLME (Yorkshire)

Lindholme has always been a Royal Air Force airfield, but in 1958 technical and storage facilities were provided here for Strategic Air Command's 7th Air Division. These were administered by the 3916th Air Base Squadron.

MANSTON (Kent)

Manston's position made it an important base for fighter escort operations during the Second World War, and in the summer of 1950 it was decided to transfer the airfield to the US 3rd Air Division. The first USAF unit to move in, in July 1950, was the 7512th Air Base Group, although American units which were subsequently based there came under the control of No. 11 Group, RAF Fighter Command. The first operational USAF unit to arrive at Manston, in July 1950, was the 20th Fighter-Bomber Wing with Republic F-84E Thunderjets, and this was followed in January 1951 by the 31st Fighter Escort Wing, which in turn was replaced by the 12th Fighter Escort Wing in June. A permanent USAF search and rescue facility was also set up at Manston from April 1951 with the arrival of the 9th Air Rescue Squadron, operating SA-16 Albatross and SB-29 Flying Fortress aircraft.

Strategic Air Command relinquished control of Manston in

November 1951, whereupon the base was taken over by the 3rd AF, USAFE. For the next few months Manston was the home of the 123rd Fighter-Bomber Wing of the Kentucky Air Guard, operating F-84Es; this was one of the units mobilised as a result of the Korean War, but it was deactivated in July 1952 and its aircraft were used to reform the 512th, 513th and 514th Fighter-Bomber Squadrons of the 406th Fighter-Bomber Wing. In November 1953 this unit became the first in Britain to receive the F-86 Sabre and its designation was changed to Fighter Interceptor Wing; at the same time the 9th Air Rescue Squadron detachment was expanded and redesignated the 66th Air Rescue Squadron. In November 1954 the 512th Fighter Squadron moved to Soesterberg in Holland and its place at Manston was taken four months later by the 92nd Fighter Squadron from Bentwaters. The 406th Fighter Interceptor Wing remained at Manston until it was deactivated in May 1958, after which the airfield reverted to RAF control.

MARHAM (Norfolk)

Marham's postwar association with the USAF began in the spring of 1946, when seven B-17 Flying Fortresses and three B-29 Superfortresses were based there for Project Ruby, which involved deep-penetration bombing trials. In June 1947 Marham was visited by nine B-29s of the 97th Bomb Group, and later that year three B-29s were based here for bombing trials against the Farge U-Boat pens. From July 1948 the airfield was used by Strategic Air Command for B-29 units on rotation from the USA, including the 307th Bombardment Group (370th and 371st Bomb Squadrons) from July until October 1948 and the 97th BG (340th and 341st BS) from November 1948 until February 1949, after which the RAF resumed control of the base.

MILDENHALL (Suffolk)

Mildenhall became an important Strategic Air Command base in July 1950 when, as a result of the Korean War emergency, the 93rd Bomb Group's 329th Bomb Squadron arrived with B-50Ds. They stayed until February 1951 when they were replaced by the 509th Bomb Group, the unit that had been specially formed to drop the atomic bomb on Japan six years earlier; other Bomb Groups rotating through Mildenhall in 1951 were the 2nd and 22nd. In August 1953 Mildenhall became a primary flight refuelling base with the arrival of KC-97E tankers, and in 1959 it assumed Burtonwood's role as the principal Military Air Transport Service transatlantic terminal under the control of the 322nd Air Division. During this period B-47s also used Mildenhall at intervals on Reflex Alert deployments. In 1966 the 513th Troop Carrier Wing arrived from Evreux, France, together with Silk Purse Control, which was the European Command's airborne command post facility. In July 1968 the controlling unit was redesignated 513th Tactical Airlift Wing, which assumed responsibility for all base functions including aircraft maintenance and the upkeep of the airborne command posts for EC-135s.

Over the years Mildenhall has seen transport aircraft movements on a massive scale in its role as the main terminus for transatlantic flights to and from Britain and Germany. C-130 wings rotate here on a regular basis coming under the control of the 435th Tactical Airlift Group. Mildenhall is also the base of the European Tanker Task Force, which is controlled by Detachment I, 306th Strategic Wing. Like the C-130 transports, the KC-135 tankers are deployed to Mildenhall from Strategic Air Command tanker wings in the continental United States, usually for periods of six weeks. Mildenhall is also used by Lockheed SR-71 and TR-1 reconnaissance aircraft.

MOLESWORTH (Cambridgeshire)

The second of the USAF's cruise missile bases in the UK, Molesworth's association with the Americans began in July 1951, when a new runway was laid down and other airfield modifications were carried out. Operations began in February 1954 with the arrival of the 582nd Air Resupply Group with twelve B-29As, four SA-16A Albatross amphibians, three

C-119Cs, and a C-47. The primary role of this unit was to provide search and rescue facilities for crews of reconnaissance aircraft which might have been forced down in hostile territory. The B-29s remained operational until October 1956 when the 582nd ARG was re-designated the 42nd Troop Carrier Squadron (Medium) under the control of USAFE. More C-119Cs were added to the strength, as well as some C-54s. Other visitors to Molesworth in the 1950s included some B-45s of the 47th Bomb Wing and WB-50 weather reconnaissance aircraft. The airfield was deactivated in December 1957 but returned to operational use in the 1980s as a cruise missile complex.

PRESTWICK (Ayrshire)

As the terminal of the North Atlantic ferry route Prestwick was extensively used by USAF and US Navy transport aircraft in the late 1940s, but it was not until 1951 that the wartime USAF base there was reactivated to provide support facilities for the Military Air Transport Service and also to give air-sea rescue coverage over the eastern Atlantic. The resident air-sea rescue unit was the 67th ARS, which left for Spain in 1966.

SCAMPTON (Lincolnshire)

During the period of the Berlin Airlift Scampton was one of the RAF bases made available to the US government, and thirty B-29 Superfortresses of the 28th Bomb Group were based here between July and October 1948. This unit was replaced by the 301st Bomb Group, which returned to the USA in January 1949 following the relaxation of international tension. Scampton subsequently returned to RAF control, although the 3930th Air Base Squadron was based there for a brief period in 1952.

SCULTHORPE (Norfolk)

The first American unit to operate from Sculthorpe post-War was the 92nd Bomb Group, which arrived in February 1949 with its B-29s. In August that year the base became the home of the first B-50As to be stationed in Britain, those of the 63rd Squadron of the 43rd Bomb Group. During the years that followed many Strategic Air Command Bomb Groups rotated through Sculthorpe on Temporary Duty, among them the 2nd, 22nd, 97th and 301st. Until January 1951 Sculthorpe had been under RAF control, but it then came under USAF administration and on 31 May 1952 B-45 Tornado jet bombers of the 84th and 85th Squadrons, 47th Bomb Group, flew in to become permanent residents. A third Squadron, the 86th, formed here in March 1954. In May that year Sculthorpe received another resident unit, the 19th Tactical Reconnaissance Squadron, whose RB-45Cs were tasked with night photographic reconnaissance, while another permanent unit to arrive in 1954 was the 8554th Tow Target Flight with TB-26B Invader target tugs and L-5 Sentinels.

As well as the front line units Sculthorpe housed the HQ of the 49th Air Division, whose C-119s, C-47s, L-20s and T-33s provided transport and communications support for the USAF's tactical forces in Britain. In January 1958 the RB-45Cs of the 19th Squadron were replaced by RB-66s, and soon afterwards B-66s also replaced the Tornados of the 47th Wing; a support tanker force was provided by KB-50D and KB-50J Superfortresses, which remained operational at Sculthorpe until March 1964. In June 1962 the 47th Bomb Wing was deactivated but Sculthorpe was retained by the USAF as a standby base. In 1985 Detachment I of the 48th Tactical Fighter Wing was based there.

SEALAND (Clwyd)

In the 1950s Sealand was used as a storage annexe to the main USAF supply base at Burtonwood. The Americans remained until August 1957, when an RAF maintenance unit was re-established there.

SHEPHERD'S GROVE (Suffolk)

In August 1951, soon after it was reactivated as a USAF base, Shepherd's Grove received the first F-86A Sabres to be based in Britain. These aircraft belonged to the 116th Squadron of the 81st Fighter Interceptor Wing, and they were joined shortly afterwards by aircraft of the 92nd Squadron. It was the first time that foreign aircraft had been assigned to the air defence of Great Britain, the aircraft coming under the control of No. 12 Fighter Group, RAF. In November 1952 the 116th Squadron was redesignated 78th Fighter Squadron, and in April 1954 its designation changed yet again to the 78th Fighter-Bomber Squadron, the reason for the change becoming apparent when the squadron began to receive F-84F Thunderstreaks later in the year. The 78th moved to Woodbridge in December 1958 and soon afterwards work began on the building of a Thor missile site for RAF Bomber Command.

STANSTED (Essex)

In the early 1950s the USAF laid plans to operate jet aircraft from Stansted and in 1954 the 803rd US Engineering Aviation Battalion began work on building a new runway with associated hard standings. The work continued until December 1956 and the engineers left Stansted in the following April, but by the summer of 1958 the Americans had decided that they no longer wished to make use of the airfield except in the event of war.

UPPER HEYFORD (Oxfordshire)

Upper Heyford's long association with the USAF began in June 1950, when various support units moved in to prepare the base for eventual use by Strategic Air Command; the airfield was formally handed over to the USAF in May 1951 when it passed under the administrative control of the 7509th Air Base Squadron. Alterations to the main runway were completed by the end of 1951, when the KB-29Ps of the 93rd Air Refuelling Squadron arrived at the start of a ninety-day operational deployment. For the next two years Upper Heyford remained primarily a flight refuelling base, being used by the KB-29 and KB-50 tankers that were responsible for flight refuelling the 97th, 509th, 2nd and 301st Bomb Groups on rotation to British bases.

The airfield was used by B-47 and RB-47 Stratojets from June 1953, and these aircraft remained Upper Heyford's principal users until March 1965 when, together with other British bases, it was transferred from SAC to USAFE. For just over a year it was maintained as a Dispersed Operating Base by the 7514th Combat Support Group, which was deactivated on the arrival of the 66th Tactical Reconnaissance Wing from France in September 1966. This unit operated RF-101C Voodoos and RF-4C Phantoms until April 1970, when it too was deactivated. Upper Heyford subsequently became the home of the 20th Tactical Fighter Wing with F-111Es, and this unit remains the base's present day occupant. The 20th TFW comprises the 55th, 77th and 79th Tactical Fighter Squadrons.

WELFORD (Berkshire)

In September 1955 after three years on Care and Maintenance, Welford reopened as a logistics site for the US 3rd Air Force, and was still used as such in 1985.

WETHERSFIELD (Essex)

After five years on Care and Maintenance, Wethersfield was taken over by the Americans in the early 1950s and the main runway lengthened. In June 1952 the 20th Fighter Group flew in with its Republic F-84G Thunderjets after a transatlantic flight via Labrador and Iceland. In February 1955 the unit's designation changed to the 20th Fighter-Bomber Wing and later in the year the Thunderjets began to be replaced by F-84F Thunderstreaks. These were followed in the summer of 1957 by F-100 Super Sabres, and in 1958 the unit was renamed the 20th Tactical Fighter Wing. Another resident unit at this time was the 23rd Helicopter Squadron with its H-21Bs for rescue and fire fighting.

The 20th TFW left Wethersfield early in 1970 to re-equip with F-111s at Upper Heyford, and in April 1970 Wethersfield was taken over by the 66th Combat Support Group. In August 1976, after being successively designated the 66th Combat Support Squadron and then Operation Location A, 10th Tactical Reconnaissance Wing, the former 66th CSG became Detachment I, 10th Tactical Reconnaissance Wing, RAF Wethersfield. Its principal role remains support and administration, and in 1985 it was accompanied at Wethersfield by the 819th Civil Engineering Squadron and the USAF Rapid Engineer Deployable and Heavy Operations Repair Squadron Engineer (Red Horse). The task of this unit is to undertake runway repairs on behalf of the 3rd Air Force, USAFE.

WITCHFORD (Cambridgeshire)

Having been a bomber base within the RAF's No. 3 Group during the Second World War, Witchford was used as a USAF stores depot from 1950 until 1952, but no flying took place.

WOODBRIDGE (Suffolk)

Woodbridge passed under American control in June 1952 and subsequently became the home of the 79th Fighter-Bomber Squadron of the 29th Fighter-Bomber Wing, operating first F-84Gs and later (from 1957) F-100 Super Sabres. In July 1958 the 81st Tactical Fighter Wing assumed operational control of Woodbridge and after necessary runway repairs the 78th Tactical Fighter Squadron flew in from Shepherd's Grove with its

F-84 Thunderstreaks. These were soon relinquished for F-101 Voodoos which the 81st TFW operated until it began to receive its first F-4 Phantoms in March 1966. Late in 1969 the 79th TFS moved to Upper Heyford, leaving the 78th TFS at Wood-bridge with F-4D Phantoms. The move made room for the arrival of the 67th Aerospace Rescue and Recovery Squadron from Moron Air Force Base in Spain with HC-130 Hercules and HH-3E 'Jolly Green Giant' helicopters. This unit occupied Woodbridge in 1985, together with the 78th and 91st Tactical Fighter Squadrons of the 81st Tactical Fighter Wing with A-10A Thunderbolt IIs.

Index

INDEX